On Belay

Adventures in Mountaineering On Two Continents

M.G. Anderson

authorHOUSE®

AuthorHouse™
1663 Liberty Drive
Bloomington, IN 47403
www.authorhouse.com
Phone: 1-800-839-8640

First published by AuthorHouse   5/29/2009

ISBN: 978-1-4389-5798-2 (sc)

Library of Congress Control Number: 2009902324

Printed in the United States of America
Bloomington, Indiana

This book is printed on acid-free paper.

What you are getting;

Is a collection of climbing tales from the ancient of days on the hills to the modern, from hobnailers to banana-shaped rock shoes if you like. It's a random troll from memory's treasure chest, and that as we all know tends to dodge and weave about perilously, forgets the rainy days, and sometimes the weft gets so warped we lose the thread of the yarn. But if memory does serve me right the true stories are pretty true, though they might not stand up in a court of law and even the fiction commences with a truth, in incidents occurring to my friends or me.

Not every story has to do with climbing. At one stage I toyed with squeezing them into the frame by tossing in some such sentence as, "It was a week after we had been to Kintail, and climbed that El-Dorado of peaks, Lladhar Bheinn." Or "He forgot now why he had put his rope and rucksack into the boot." But that smacks of cheating, and while we have all held onto that runner longer than we needed to it's not something we want to make a habit.

Mountaineering in all its myriad forms has been the all-encompassing experience of my life, all-consuming too. One thinks of the aroma of wet anoraks and breeches tediously drying out from Monday to next Friday, wafting a pungent and persistent reminder of the day on the hill. Note I did not say 'all consuming *passion*.' Too many wet weekends in Wales can temporarily dampen the ardour of the most fervent hill lover, but the addiction is incurable, and let's face it makes you wonder how normal people spend their weekends.

As a guarantee of authenticity, the author has previously climbed all the mountains, and climbing routes that form the stories' background. That is I should say all bar one. But even here veracity is as good as preserved for all but the most severe pedants, as the hero fails to do the route.

There are ghost stories, a murder mystery, and tales of love gone wrong. So there's something for everyone.

Any resemblance to any living character is entirely coincidental, with the exception of the true stories where you can really point the finger. By the way in case any one is thinking of calling the *polis*, I didn't break into The Scottish mountaineering Club hut in Glencoe. Therein lies a reference to a *cause celebre* of the 60s that provoked much comment at the time, but now is of mere antediluvian interest. In at least one of the stories the chronological setting is all-askew. The climbing equipment references are to the sixties but the story had to be placed in the nineties for reasons that will be obvious to the reader.

Good luck and enjoy.

Gavin Anderson

On Belay......... Foreword

Mountaineering has one of the richest literatures of any sport, and some of its classic tales such as Joe Simpson's 'Touching the Void' have become books appreciated by a much wider audience than just climbers.

Reading the stories in this volume I have the same anticipation about their appeal. Essays such as 'Green Go', 'The Marquis of Kettlewell', and 'Tiptoe through the Treetops' have little or nothing to do with mountains, but say much about the human condition.

However Gavin Anderson is an active climber, and is known in the sport as a 'Lifer'. That is someone who is in the game, whatever, for the whole of their existence. And thus he is a mountaineer with wide experience of the activity. Beginning in his native Scotland, and other UK climbing centres, he has subsequently climbed and travelled from the Alps to the Andes.

The stories in 'On Belay' are in some cases humorous, others are gripping! They are very inventive and written in a most appealing and frank style, revealing much about the BIG personality of their author.

I first read an essay by Gavin in the Scottish Mountaineering Club Journal, and I remember thinking at the time that 'this guy really can write, he should publish a book of such stories!' And now he has done just that, and they are of a truly memorable and idiosyncratic style. Therefore I am happy to recommend them to be read by one and all!

Dennis Dillon Gray........ Leeds 25th February 2009.

Contents

"Warning, Ice!"

A tale of climbing in the golden age.

"Come outside. It's incredible!" Dave, a naturalized Scot by way of Wolverhampton, whose scenic wonders were an acquired taste, was standing in the entrance to the hut. I clumped out and gasped thick white steam in cold astonishment. In front of us the vast Moor of Rannoch was ablaze in a glory of gold and purple. A few tiny limpid clouds lingered like smoke on the flat plain. All the rest of the sky was a bright steely blue. On our right the rocks of the Buchaille were light pink, smeared in white. A few patches of mint green were the telltale signs of ice, wonderful, reassuringly climbable ice.

From this angle the Buchaille was not the perfect melodious triangle seen from the road over the moor, but rather an imposing lump, almost self-satisfied as if saying, "I know I am not perfect from all angles, but I am quite happy the way I am." Or it was as if the divine sculptor had created a masterpiece from one angle and then nodded off.

We cramponed up the lower slope of Crowberry Gully unroped. Steep brick-red walls of rock hemmed in our great white way up the mountain. The spikes on our feet, the axe and spiked peg hammers in our hands formed four adhesive claws in the cement-hard snow. It was the best of conditions in the golden days of yore, and it was my first outing on steep ice. After our first careless stomp up the gully, I had happened to glance between my legs. The slope, steep and featureless, went a long way down to end in a sheer cliff. A slip here would be curtains. I wanted to put the rope on, but I was stubborn or cowardly enough to wait until Dave suggested it.

"We might as well rope up and belay to this." So saying he slapped his axe against what looked like a road sign standing upright in the middle of the gully.

"What's on it?" I said in crisp, panting smoke signals.

"It says," He scraped the frost and snow off the board, "Beware Ice!"

I knew that the major ice pitches were above us, so it must have been placed in this off road position by a mountaineering prankster. "How on earth did it get up here?"

"It was one of the Creagh Dhu after a ceilidh in the Kingshouse."

"You mean he brought it up here alone and at night?"

"Sure. And he soloed the rest of the gully afterwards. He said it got harder because the road sign was the best ice axe he'd ever had."

"I don't believe a word of it."

"Neither do I." He held out the ropes, "Just look after these."

Belayed to the signpost while Dave led up the slope, I was more relaxed, the only disturbance to my inner karma were dribbles of snow he kicked down all managing to funnel themselves malevolently under my collar to give the back of my neck a miserable time. Soon I was following him with the rope lightly teasing me upwards. On reaching the stance, I kicked a wee resting spot, let him adjust the rope and then I was off in front. Boldly leading into the unknown, I gasped to myself while kicking my feet hard into the snow. The weapons in my hands were

2

bashed instinctively into the slightly blue-tinged white stuff. I felt more than a tremor of alarm. My heart was palpitating wildly and my throat went dry. Dave's reassuring voice down the slope, only served to make me aware of how far he was below me. Once I made the mistake of turning round to ask him what he had just said. I was miles above him! If I came off and shot down the slope, the jerk of the rope would pull him off, no bother, and both of us would be hurled into oblivion. Not for the first time I realized that an imagination was not always a blessing. I clung to the slope and started hacking a hole in the snow for a stance and belay. I ignored Dave's cheery shout that I could go for another 50 feet as there was plenty of rope left. That was the way it went on. He led out 150 feet and I relaxed, climbed up to him and then climbed above him in increasingly diminishing rope lengths. It never occurred to me that our fates would be identical if he came tippling down. Everything seemed safer when he was in charge.

Dave was now ensconced at the bottom of a boulder-choked bottleneck chimney.

"Lucky you. You've got the first ice pitch," he said. I gave a quick look to see that he was solidly anchored to the mountain, and then set to work, chipping massive foot and handholds in the ice. At six feet above the belay I realized that I was going to exhaust myself. The ice was intractable and every step had to be quarried with great effort. You could never dance up this as you could on rock. It was like going a hike where you had to build your own track. I hung around trying to be decisive.

"I am coming down for a rest. Watch my rope," I shouted back over my shoulder and pivoted down from step to step. It was no use. I lacked the punch to lead the ice chimney. What with his tea cosy balaclava and his thick glasses, I could never read Dave's expression. He looked at me inscrutably, then with all the tact he could summon up said, "Mind if I have a try?" Selflessly I stood aside. Quickly he surmounted my staircase, then neatly, economically and confidently cut neat little holds all the way to the snow above. Going up I wondered if I would ever climb ice or would always be a passenger. Transferring from my messy holds to his perfect little niches was a minor embarrassment, reminding me of the accursed splodges of my handwriting, set beside the neat chastisement of my teachers'. "Take more care!"

Above us the gully forked. Our route swept away to the right over ice-coated slabs. I anchored the belay securely at the junction. From where I stood the ice draped slabs, steeper than a church steeple, glinted maliciously, hard and unyielding as adamant. Below Dave's feet the slope tilted dizzily down to our footsteps of an hour ago, now forlorn and remote, as he tapped hand and footholds, steadily and surely as a crab on a familiar shore. Hardly a breath of wind disturbed the cold-sheeted ice, although an occasional snow devil spun crazily around the burnished red retaining walls. Framed in between them I could see the slopes of Beinn a'Chrulaiste opposite, spring-coloured in the sun, almost calling out, 'What are you doing in that miserable chill dungeon?' Now and then, in a controlled steady voice Dave said, 'Mind the rope'. I noticed that a tear line of mottled dashes of sea-blue punctuated the immaculate white of the slope where his steps had punctured the ice.

After a while he disappeared round the corner, his progress marked by lumps of excavated ice whirring and whistling downwards. A bit later I heard, "C'mon up," and the ropes tugged insistently upwards. "Keep the ropes tight." My stiff, iced-up mitts were sticky in the handholds. An occasional wipe with my glove sufficed to clear the holds from the constant dribbles of snow that kept filling them up. Safe and suspended like a puppet, I had to admire his boldness when forced to fumble about groping blindly for footholds.

"Well done, a really great lead," I burbled enthusiastically on reaching the frozen alcove he had excavated for a belay. "Aye well, you've got a better pitch coming," he said stamping his feet round the little sentry box to keep warm, till underfoot was like a pepper pot. I looked up at the intimidating wall of ice above broken by a cave high up on the left wall, then like a mad miner, I chopped a staircase of massive coalscuttle steps up into the cave, "I'll belay here." Dave came up to me in a series of confident bunny hops, his balaclava totally covered with snow even up to the silly little red bobble on the top. By now the day's early sparkle was replaced by more sombre tones, a sure sign of the imminence of darkness in Scotland's short winter days.

Up the hanging wall of ice he went. Tucked away in the grotto I was safe from the snow and ice lumps knocked down. With no breeze to chill the body it was almost warm and for the first time since putting on crampons this morning, I felt totally safe with my ropes tied off round massive icy stalactites. In the ice cave the subdued greenish-blue light was very similar to being underwater in Portobello swimming pool.

Soon it was my turn to step out from the safety of the cave. Immediately I felt exposed on the sheer ice. I forced my fingers deep into the icy grips. My boots scraped about for their holds as if the crampons were antennae. I could have looked to see if my feet were properly placed, but as this involved peering down and the concomitant horrors of gazing into the abyss, I ended up scraping and threshing with my feet till every now and then, by luck, my foot found one hold and then another. By approximating to the rhythm of Dave's stride I more or less managed to keep to his footpath, but my heart still skipped a beat whenever I missed a step.

"Keep that rope tight!" Then. "Really tight." My anxious plea turned into a half shriek when I thought I was parting company with the slope.

Every time I opened my mouth it was filled with spin-drift. Luckily Dave kept the rope tighter than a corset. Imperceptibly the angle lessened; the unremitting ice turned to more obliging snow. I progressed upwards with added assistance from elbows and knees, and from there it was a short easy trek to the summit.

We unroped, and then sauntered down, axes under our arms and crampons occasionally sparking on exposed stones. The sun was setting in a thin scarf of pale fire. We paid it a brief contented homage before we sank into the shadows of Llagangarbh Corrie. Halfway down, the slope eased. Gratefully we took off our crampons and glissaded back down towards the hut, whooping and shrieking with delight. It had been a great day - a classic day we would remember when we were toasting our toes in front of the fire and bragging to our bairn's bairns about a once upon a time Scotland, when men put salt on their porridge.

Nae Mair Black Bun

"You dinnae like Hogmanay? Ca' yersel a Scot?" My interlocutor paused to summon up all his reserves of amazement and contempt. Telling him that more days are lost to British Industry through alcohol etc, would have been a waste of breath. Besides I was used to being impugned for this heresy. If I am guilty of rejecting Scotland's civilisation at her zenith, so be it, but after one 31st December, when I walked along Rose Street, saw the drunks stretched head to toe in the gutter, and witnessed the bad-tempered fights between friends fuelled by the "fiery creatur," I decided enough was enough, although, one of the accessories to this festivity almost makes it all worth-while. I am talking of Black Bun, that fruity concoction of sultanas and flies cemetery, which makes its fleeting appearance at this unhallowed hour.

I was planning to sip a quiet dram, bite down a bit of black bun and retire to bed, before friends in the Edinburgh JMCS, proud new owners of the Auld Smiddy in Dundonnell, invited me to join them. The offer of a retreat from the hullabaloo of Hogmanay, to the unsullied wilderness of Torridon was too good to refuse, so off we went. When we arrived, people were already settling in, laying out their sleeping bags, bagging the best places, everyone laughing, even some singing, Glen Campbell's

"Galveston," for no apparent reason; the usual high spirits at the beginning of a promising weekend. A homely glow was provided by the old furnace, crackling and creaking in a most satisfactory manner, but after years of disuse, prodding the blocked chimney with ice axes simply increased the general stour in the air, so that a smoky layer of cumulo-nimbus clouds nestled above the top bunks with the result that at the end of the weekend we went home with sooty faces, hair clogged with carbon, the auld grey heids a lot happier and all of us coughing intermittently.

But even here, amidst the wild, craggy, splendours of the Western Highlands, the obligations of New Year couldn't be evaded. The locals, purely out of old-fashioned Highland hospitality, had invited us to bring it in *a la Gaeltacht*, so that even I, the Hogmanay hermit, could hardly refuse without appearing selfish and discourteous.

Stepping outside the howff, was a pleasant relief from the choke-damp within, the frost on the roof of the Smiddy a glittering white carapace under a crisp, starry sky. When we entered the hotel, still coughing and spluttering, no one greeted us. Lined up in front of the bar in an assortment of deerstalkers and flat caps, each hat sporting a medly of fishing flies, stood an almost motionless rank of drinkers for all the world like a congregation at prayer. There was no hum of conversation, only a few indistinct orders breaking through the slurping and clinking. Any Englishman happening on this still life would assume this was Scotland at its dourest; the toper's version of Sunday in the Kirk, but this was purely preparatory. Every man jack of them was busily injecting the required tonnage of booze into his system, to get the requisite head of steam for an arduous night ahead. The muffled orders gradually distilled themselves. There was "Pint O'heavy an' a hauf, Jimmy" or simply "hauf'n heavy, Jimmy." Jimmy was moving like a whippet from end to end of the bar, dispensing refreshment without pause or interval. All the taps were on, and when one glass was filled its place was taken by a clean glass with ne'er a drop of spillage. And it was a clean glass. There was no malingering of the sort that you sometimes get, "In the same glass, then?" There was no doubt Jimmy was the hero of the year's end, the Stakhanov of the Bar.

Towards ten, the tempo increased to a frenzy. People were ordering double, treble and even quadruple rounds as the hour of doom approached, when the shutters would clang down on that awful final note. Would we all be flung out at closing time, forgotten by our hosts, and have to celebrate by the frozen Lochside? This question was forgotten when our genial host - not Jimmy; he was merely a superior factotum - appeared to announce, "Ben the Hoose."

Once ensconced in the best room, my social sloth took over, so I slunk into a remote armchair, but even hiding in a corner, couldn't stop the torrent of whisky coming at me from all directions. A few nips was enough to tell me, I had more than enough. Refusal was pointless; when my glass was half full, for mine host it was half empty. Putting my hand over the rim didn't staunch the deluge either. They simply poured over it. Luckily there was a pot plant nearby. Nobody took any notice my watering it with pure spirit, but later, when I became an environmentalist, I felt guilty about that sozzled flower.

The return to the Smiddy was unmemorable, that is to say I have no memory of it. Getting into my pit was awkward, but eventually both legs were in and bodily logistics taken care of, I immediately fell asleep.

I was awoken by the first light of day peeking timidly through the slats of the shuttered door, as it slowly creaked open. Figures were creeping about in the shaft of dusty light coming from the doorway. A louder creak sent a spasm shuddering through my head, my hangover's First Footing.

"A Guid New Year tae yin'n aw !"

Silence.

"Are ye a' deid?"

More of the above.

Three locals, who had missed out on the party, were doing some catching up. Everyone was asleep or dozing half awake, struggling to return to it. Nobody answered their genial salutations. One of them giving up this thankless task, sat down on a stool in the middle of the Smiddy and within a moment collapsed into drunken slumber. The other two split their forces; one Gaelic Goliath dished out cheer to the top deck, while the other catered to the lower bunk. They offered refreshment from their New Year bottles, shook hands or in the case of the girls sealed the moment with a Gaelic snog. As far as I could make out most people blearily complied, even though the liquor must have tasted quite revolting on their heavily encrusted tongues. The Highlanders were fairly forceful with their greetings. Refusing "To tak' a New Year," was asking for trouble. Several slumbering climbers were shaken into the New Year anew and much whisky gurgled its merry way down reluctant throats. The sleeping damosels clearly were not enjoying the mauling they were getting; but if their boyfriends were too spineless to intervene, they had better just lie back and think of Scotland.

Two along from me a girl was weeping miserably as the drunken giant plied her with festive cheer. It would be my turn soon. I dived down leaving only my nose poking through as a snorkel. A pointless exercise for pretty soon my draw-cord was tugged open to reveal a visage that was to provide material for my nightmares for years to come, worse than the worst hairiest Heelander in Braveheart. For no reason at all I found myself talking in an uptight voice as if I had spent my formative years at Fettes. "No, thank you so much. I have had quite enough to drink and now, my good man, if you wouldn't mind letting me go to sleep. We have a long day on the hill, tomorrow, or rather today, and unless I get to sleep right away, there won't be time for brekkers, and I can't imagine there will be any place of refreshment open this Ne'erday to supplement our rations."

"Hey Feargus, jusht listen at this English Pfluff. 'No law de daw plaice o'ar Refreshment open todaih'. Listen, Twala," he roared, "jusht stuff this boattle, sorry *supplementary ration* doon your place o' refreshment or I'll mak ye remember Prestonpans." He grabbed my sleeping bag jack-knifing me upright, just as I was wondering why anyone from South of Loch Lomond is immediately suspected of Englishry.

"Get a dram of the Fiery Cratur in yer belly and ye won't need tae stoap for refreshment. Ye, Mealy Pudden!"

"Well, if perchance you have some of that delicious black bun, I could entertain a nibble."

"A nibble, *Ooh entertain a nibble!* I'll gie ye a nibble! We've nay mair black bun, an' if we had I'd ram it up your Sassenach erse! Noo tak yer dram!"

"Maybe he disnae want ane." This voice of reason came from the lower deck.

"Whit?"

His chum, Feargus, was upholding a less rigorous standard of enforcement in sharing the cup that cheers, perhaps being less of a lion-hearted patriot than his pal, or possessed of that other powerful national characteristic, being canny with his bawbees. I couldn't help noticing the bottle about to be rammed between my teeth, was a twelve year old MacAllan, entirely wasted on the furred up tongues of the libatees.

"Haud on, Donhail. I tellt ye. Leave the laddie alane."

"Whit? He'll tak his New Year like a man."

"Go on gie him a break. He doesnae want yer whisky. C'mon doon."

"Whit?"

"He doesnae want it."

"We'll He's goin' tae get it!"

"Leave him alane!"

"Awa'n bile yer heid!"

"Whit?" - A favourite word of theirs; now played back by Fergus.

"He'll tak his New Year."

"No he winnae! Lets awa hame tae oor beds."

"Feargus, awa and bile yer heid!"

"Whit?" A dangerous pause. "Nae-yin tells me to bile ma heid!"

"Well am tellin' ye the noo. Awa an' bile it wi a sheep's heid an'a!"

"Whit!" This was Feargus in case you're losing track.

At that moment all extraneous noise was drowned out as the bottle was upended against my tonsils, and in order to prevent death by drowning I had to swallow the whisky to the last drop.

"Yer a real Scotsman, noo!" was the last bulletin from mine unwanted host, as his legs were dragged down off the bunk by his inflamed friend. Desperately Donhail scratched for some purchase on the edge of the bunk. Captured in the glimmering fire light was a *Kilroy Was Here* cartoon figure peeking over the bunk, except this one had a raggedy beard, with an expression trapped midway between surprise and anguish.

"And let me wish you a Happy New Year!" I shouted festively.

"Whit?" And Kilroy disappeared from view.

This "Whit" was Donhail's Farewell to Dundonnell as Feargus was about to demonstrate precisely his objections to boiling his head. Now preferring action to words, Feargus took off his jacket and threw it at the third member. "Hector haud that," which jacket plopped over Hector's heedless head, making him a sleeping coat-rack.

Down below, there were three loud cracks followed by, "Ye'll no tell me to bile ma heid!" The brawl was brief. Feargus was a bonny fechter, and briskly sorted out the attempted enforcer. Besides Donhail was not allowed to take his jacket off, which was stuck midway, half on, half off, impeding efficient combat. Unfair perhaps, but these Highlanders never learned to play cricket.

The commotion at last managed to wake up Hector, the third reveler. He was completely taken aback, blindfolded in addition to being befuddled by drink.

"Whair am I? Turn on the light! Mah e'en, mah e'en!" He shrieked panicstricken. "Help! I've been blinded. I've lost mah sight! Oh Jings! I should have never hae drunk yon porridge whisky at the bothan!"

He rushed about the Smiddy and I watched in fascination as he smacked straight into the anvil with a horribly painful crack then neatly pole-vaulted over it. He looked about him like a lost dog. The jacket-cum-blindfold had fallen onto the floor. Silence. He touched his eyes. "It's a miracle! It's a New Year miracle! I was blind and now I can see! See?" He pointed to his eyes in case anyone was interested, and limped out at a run.

"I'm going to the kirk right noo. Whaur is it?" Far away I just caught him practising his New Year Resolution: "I'll never, Meenester. I'll never touch a drop again. So help ma, Boab. No hooch onyway."

....

As sometimes happens Ne'erday turned out to be extremely fine, bringing with it the promise of a bright fresh new start, kissing goodbye to the lame half-life of mediocrity and failure of the previous twelve months, a delusion lasting as long as snow in the Lake District. There was a fiery lurid dawn of orange and yellow cloud, while we tramped the frozen bog to the foot of the ridge. So far it was like any of a hundred grey days in the hills. Another day, another set of wet clothes. Mounting up to the shoulder of the ridge the team was sucked into a thick clammy mist. The wind blew; the wet drizzle spat in our faces, Hunching down into our anoraks, we resigned ourselves to another dreary outing. Sheets of mist billowed down in long columns, each one damper than the last, first grey, then brighter sparkling with little sequins. An Teallach, clad in veils of swirling mist, coyly wrapped up, then slowly revealing all, a stone Salome, its gorgeous towers uncannily bringing to mind the first sighting of Dracula's castle in an old Hammer Horror Movie.

Then all petty thoughts disappeared as the mist boiled away and evaporated, and a glorious winter sun took over. All the regrets, the melancholies of the past year were burnt out in that spectacular array. Set in front were row upon row of pinnacles, crags and battlements glistening white giants' milk teeth under a cloudless sky, the snow, a flawless satin, so bright that even with sunglasses, we had to turn from the mountains and look to the plain for relief. In contrast with the monochrome heights, the heather, gorse and broom of the lowland provided a patchwork of amethyst browns and greens, fragmented by a myriad of startling blue lochans stretching towards the horizon where it melted into the snow whitened hills. To the west the Atlantic shimmered in a calm sea broken only by the Summer Isles, rubies in a sapphire setting.

Nothing could disturb our harmony with the mountain that day. Surmounting the brow we all whooped in exultation, voices carrying easily in the still air; even the creak of crampons and the snap of crisply crackling snow could be heard clearly. No other human sounds disturbed the calm. Brushing snow off the handholds, we discovered the rock, warm and dry within minutes; the midwinter sun hotter than on many a summer day.

The climbing itself was beyond perfection, *neve* safe, solid and plastic, giving technically interesting moves in a situation of apparent drama, but well-secured with ropes and runners. Balancing and tiptoeing over spikes, spillikins and gendarmes, we peeked into a never-ending series of delights, snow covered bushman's huts and pot kilns all in a line, the towers, bulbous haystacks out of a painting by Courbet. Sitting on the Leaning Tower known as Lord Berkeley's Seat, with all around us the lavish splendour of a winter's day in the Northern Highlands, mountain upon mountain varnished with silver, strewn about in prodigal abundance, the thought occurred that if there was a magic carpet, there was nowhere else to be, not even the Karakorum. The little breeze that had sprung up when the trip started died away. A century ago Mummery, atop the Matterhorn, noted the air was so still that cigarette smoke ascended directly heavenwards. None of us smoked to put it to the test but today would have been such a day.

Too soon we left behind the last ice-crusted pinnacle and descended to a grand sloping plateau, wind polished into a silvery mirror, its surface transformed into burnished gold by the lowering sun, which dropping behind the ocean set the Atlantic afire with molten red. On that last slope down to the Smiddy the dusk air turned chilly and lifeless as if the sun's going had switched the magic off.

Minutes later we were in the hut chattering away over a warming brew and hot soup, the cold forgotten, a row of blue-flamed primuses purring away like happy kittens; dixies on the boil dancing, and everyone burbling away in the *joie de vivre* of this paradisiacal day. Each team coming in had given their verdict. We had been dancing with the gods and angels in the Empyreum. No one exactly said that, the English language failing miserably to meet the demands put upon it, so we had to fall back on hackneyed expressions of exuberance for this once in a lifetime day on the hill, as in "Whit a great day!" Absolutely trounced by, "It was better than a fish supper!" Bringing it down to a common experience we had all enjoyed. One bright spark, who fancied himself as being in touch with the great world outside, came out with, "It was better than a fish supper when WH Murray dined alone." But this was met by deservedly blank stares all around.

Or so they all told me. I was part of that ecstatic crew only by proxy. My great day had been spent, head over a bucket clenched between my knees inspecting my very own Jackson Pollock therein; my headache thumping away to a perpetual, "Galveston," while afar off, as if in a distant glen, my stomach was erupting on a diminishing ration of nutrients.

And you wonder why I avoid Hogmanay?

Glen of Weeping

I swear this happened to me. It was early in '92. You probably remember it was one of those no winter winters. It could have been a touch of machismo or more likely masochism that persuaded me to pitch my tent on Gunpowder Green at the foot of the Buchaille for the week, and I wanted to brag to the lads that we were climbing in shirtsleeves on the Rannoch Wall in February in Glencoe! Truth to tell there was that little matter of breaking and entering, which I suspected the Scottish Mountaineering Club were finding hard to forgive, so I steered well clear of Llagangarbh Cottage.

Those were the great days. In my memory the rock was pink as coral, and strong and dependable like the Scottish character. High above the Moor just when you made that hard move the breeze could waft up the scent of heather, presenting a bouquet for your efforts. The Wall swept away beneath us for hundreds of feet, while the Moor stretched into the distance like a great purple lake lapping at its foot.

We did Agag's Groove treading a wary way up the front of the Rannoch Wall. The next day we climbed Grooved Arête, which was like tiptoeing quietly past your parents' bedroom after midnight, every move stealthy, almost furtive, your fingers wrapped round good clean jugs, moving up on sharp rough in-cut holds, till you felt you were gliding up the rock foot by foot, an illusion easily shattered by the occasional glance at the space beneath your feet, giving a sharp intake of breath reminder of mortality, but we were climbing well; one of those days when you felt like a winged angel.

Confidence soared. I was getting pushy; in the mood to believe if there was a route there must be holds for any mortal man. So we had to have a go at Red Slab, vaguely aware of its understated reputation. Archie tried to warn me I was pushing the boat out that this might be too much for me to handle. I got into a horrible irreversible position, and watched my hat falling off. It fluttered then was caught by a draught and disappeared. I was frutching and clutching at straws like mad. I glanced past my straining arms and saw Archie gripped out of his mind at the belay both arms hugging the rock and the rope between his teeth. The belay peg I saw moving in its socket, and his popping out eyes told me what he thought of my climbing style. A member of the Creagh Dubh, on Curved Ridge opposite, ceased in his badinage, and urgently told us to come down, so we knew it must be serious.

I lunged and landed on a hold. I had to move quickly. My hands were sweaty and my legs were bicycling against the rock. Bit by bit I got there. I was lucky; I had got away with it; all that was left were a few sweaty nightmares. Some of my friends had not been so lucky.

That night as we were supping our brew under the cold stars, Archie said he had to leave the next day. Work, or family was calling urgently. I believed him, although I thought my escapades might have jogged his conscience. As he tramped through the tufts of heather to the road, that next grey morning I waved goodbye standing by the tent, not without a touch of melancholy. Loneliness is not something I am well equipped to deal with, and it hit me as soon as he got a lift. He struck it lucky. There were few cars on the road and he thumbed down the first one to pass.

Now I was alone waiting for Ronald MacDonald. Yes, that was his name, and if you are going to read this with a straight face you will have to get past all that. Ronald couldn't, and if you remarked on it when you met him, best not to expect a laugh. So we compromised and called him Rab. Well, he was due to arrive in two days, so I had to think of things to do to fill the gap. Fortunately it rained. There is nothing worse than kicking your heels in good climbing weather with no partner. I knew Rab would turn up. He was the most reliable of the lads. His word was his bond and so forth. I had better listen to the rain drumming on the roof of the tent, and bide my time. For two days it poured. No one came and I just lay in the tent reading damp books in a damp space, breaking off to mop up the retreating island of dryness with a damp towel. Looking out I could see sheets of rain sweeping down the glen towards me. No wonder it was called the Glen of Weeping. On the third morning my toes started to feel the wet, and I started to snuffle ominously. My only companions were the sopping wet sheep, munching grass with mechanical persistence, occasionally taking a break to bleat mournfully. Apart from that they had no conversation. I stopped pretending this was an exciting adventure when a rain spot began to steadily drip through the cheesecloth covering that was my tent, landing unerringly on my face. A fly sheet was for the effete. No matter where I moved my face the drip followed me round, the Glencoe version of an ancient Chinese torture, and the next day I moved my tent to a dryer higher site, as a new tributary of the River Coe began burrowing and bubbling its way under my groundsheet. If Rab was to find me he would have a problem. So I had an idea. With my spare set of cutlery I would fashion an arrow showing the safe place to cross.

But first I had to get across the river. It appeared higher than normal so I was in for a wetting. Starkers clutching my cutlery I waded in. Ah, wasn't I just wet behind the ears then. The Coe, from being a drought starved trickle, was now in full flood. Some things you never learn till you experience them; the strength of water in spate, for example. I was whipped off my feet the instant I immersed myself in the burn. I always wondered how hydro-electricity works and now I know, I thought in a detached manner, as I was being hurtled downstream. Still thinking the daftest things, I collided into a boulder, and luckily managed to grab hold of it. It was a large boulder, about the size of a petrol drum and must have been sitting on the same spot on the streambed long before the Massacre of 1692. But now with the current tugging at a flailing man embracing it for dear life, it began to move slowly but definitely downstream for the first time in eons, just as the stones of the Parthenon moved when disturbed by rude predators. With a super-human lunge I threw myself at the bank. My hand clasped a tuft of heather, and I pulled at it. My shoulders rose out of the water. The heather gave way and I was down under again. The current threw me back up against the bank and I clawed frantically at stones embedded in it, but they were slippery, round and I could make no purchase, but then I saw a bracken root half way up the bank and in desperation cocked my feet over it, a climbing move fifteen years before its time. I threw my free hand over the top. It skidded off with no friction to impede progress. At the edge, a rough piece of granite cut my wrist and then, joy, it was in my grasp. There was no better handhold in the whole of Glencoe. I heaved and with a sucking sound emerged from the water, and rolled onto the bank. I flopped and gasped; lying in the heather letting the wind and rain lather me all over. Later I curled up, shivering in my damp sleeping bag, and tried not to think about my educational experience.

There is nowhere on Earth more beautiful than the Coe on a sunny day, and nowhere more dismal and dreich at other times. Whenever I stuck my head out of the tent, and saw dark clouds scudding across a leaden sky, depression settled over me. If the cloud lifted like a heavy blanket it was only to reveal somber dripping rocks. After a few seconds of this glum scene, it would close down again. On a day such as this, it was impossible to believe in the concept of sunshine, or that in another place and time girls in summer dresses would be laughing and eating candy floss on a warm beach, but all too easy to believe in dark supernatural forces and see in your mind's eye the serried ranks of unavenged MacDonalds drawing their spectral swords high up in the lonely glen. With a companion to chat to I could easily have shaken off this nonsense. But I had seen neither hide nor hare of another soul for days now, and the sheep, as I said, weren't much company.

I had difficulty in sleeping that night. The incessant rain had let up a little, but only to be supplanted by a stark wind that howled and whinnied as if it was dredging up the old murder victims from their unhallowed resting places. Then the soughing of the winds ceased and was replaced by a sudden blood-chilling shriek. 'It's only the wind,' I told myself without much conviction. I remembered that my grandmother's maiden name was Campbell. My mother had made a joke of this when I left. "Watch your pal, Ronald doesn't want a replay o' 1692." In that soaking tent all alone in the dark it was no joke. I checked to make sure no can of Campbell's Oxtail Soup had sneaked into my store. You don't believe I'm serious; writing this I can't believe it either, but there it is. There was also this bad habit of reading a lot. Last week I had been browsing through a volume entitled "A Horrible History of the Highlands," and found that the Massacre was only one of a series of grisly tales from that airt. If you swallowed everything you read you would spot unawakened dead strewn about like litter behind boulders, tucked into clefts in the rocks, even lying unconsecrated and unburied in the heather. No, I was not gullible but maybe a wee bit nervous. Bothies were haunted and there were tales of walkers leaving their cars and never seen again, of abandoned shielings, where strange sounds were heard in the night. The clamor of the winds battering against the tent was like a clan massacre. At one point the wind died and I could swear I heard the tread of footsteps approaching. It must have been sheep, my sanity said. But then two legged sheep?

The temperature was dropping like a stone. I resolved to leave early next morning. The reliable Rab must have got confused about the meeting place, and was now probably waiting at the other end of the Glen, near the Clachaig, the site of the old Massacre, sitting comfortably entrenched behind a pint of McEwen's Export. The more I thought about it, the more it seemed likely that Rab was at the wrong end of the valley, as he had threatened to bring an ice-axe, and there was always more snow at the West end of the Glen than by the Buchaille side. At first light my pack was ready and I headed out for the road. Visibility in the fog was virtually nil, and so remembering my near drowning, I walked a considerable way upstream till I found a rickety old bridge, I had never noticed before, and crossed it gingerly. Then the rain started again, except this time it came in the form of sleet and hail lashing me painfully. If I headed towards the road I should hit Cameron's Barn, and find some shelter in between thumbing for lifts, and maybe some Glaswegian company. Of course I hadn't got a compass, and pretty soon was aimlessly drifting about hoping to run into the road. There were still no cars, but I must be near enough to hear if any were passing. The sleet had abated somewhat, then came back again as drizzle, frugally doling out a dull light that revealed a sad washed out scene, boulders smeared in off white, grass and heather slumped under the weight of sleet and rain, and crags black and ugly. It depressed me and I felt a slight shiver as if someone had just walked over my grave.

I looked at my watch and realized I had spent a long time getting virtually nowhere for now it was early afternoon but so poor was the light it could have been nightfall, and I wasn't getting any drier. The rain stopped again, but the dampness if anything, was getting worse, with this mist seeping into everything, and it was getting colder, like a graveyard, it occurred to me. I could see about a yard in front of my nose, and that was it. In the unlikely event of a car coming when I reached the road, it was ten to one I would be knocked over. But there was no road. Had I missed seeing it and crossed over inadvertently? If so I could be somewhere in the middle of the featureless flat bog that was the middle of the Glen. Impossible to believe? Strange things happen to your mind when you are lost. I could be anywhere, even in the middle of the Moor of Rannoch if I had gone in the wrong direction. The ground underfoot was boggy enough. My mud soaked boots could testify to that. People got lost there, and found months later as a pile of bleached bones picked clean by the crows. I took off my rucksack and sat on it. It started to snow. I got up and used my sack as a shelter against the snow. I remembered that the prevailing wind in the Coe was Westerly, so if I headed upwind I would eventually reach Glencoe Village and shelter, where I was sure Rab was in the Clachaig Inn waiting on me. I carried on without much conviction, unsure of where I was going, and what I might encounter, all I really knew was that it was fatal to stay still.

I came up with a start. Right below me was the boiling torrent of The Meeting of the Three Waters, another step and I would have been in. That was a very nasty shock. And still no road. And then an odd thing. In the middle of the torrent, was an old woman standing on a bleached stone wearing what looked like three rag-tag dresses on top of one another. She was washing stuff in the river, keening mournfully to herself, while rocking back and forward on what must have been an extremely slippery stone. I shouted at her but she ignored me. Just as well, for she was clearly demented, and would probably try to wheedle money out of me and tell me my fortune. She was washing a sheet. It was a large sheet, kind of lumpy in the middle, and it passed through my head it was a shroud, which goes to show what a nervous Nellie I was. Then the blizzard closed in and shut her off from me.

Five minutes later I wasn't sure what I had seen. Ten minutes later, I convinced myself I had imagined the whole thing. I plowed on past rocks that loomed up like battleships, foaming torrents, and old sheep bones and skulls. I managed to circumvent the numerous crags in this area. You knew there was a cliff ahead, when the heather gave out onto exposed red rock.

A full-blown February blizzard, whose hard little flakes were smacking my face like bee stings and blinding me, was coming on at me now. Somewhere wretched cattle were crying out, and every now and then sheep, gaunt and scraggier than their plump upland cousins, would pop up out of the white, bleat pathetically and vanish again. Glencoe village must be close by. There was a smell of burning, which I hoped came from jolly peat fires, but which my fearful disposition persuaded me came from somewhere else. The snow let up for an instant, and for that instant I thought I was on the set of Brigadoon, but instead of the colorful anachronistic gaiety of the Hollywood Highlands lay a mean impoverished version of the same. More than money had run out.

Before me was a line of old Bothies; all made out of rough stones like the old Highland Black Houses and all in pretty shabby order, thatched with untidy slabs of peat arranged anyhow. This must be the tinkers' settlement, squalid beyond belief, every doorstop adorned with piles of shit. At the very least there was would be some shelter from the storm, and remembering the highland hospitality I had been treated to in the past, a seat by the fire followed by the quintessential dram, tea and fruitcake, I knocked and pushed aside the sacking that served for a door. Inside was pitch black, except where a flickering pitch-pine torch gave out an uncertain light. I attuned my eyes to the gloom. There was something strange about the place, hard to put your finger on; a smell I couldn't identify. Then I realized it was a smell of old greasy mutton fat and something else much nastier. Since I was standing on packed earth my feet didn't make a sound. The ground was slippery and sticky which made it feel as if it were composed of congealed muck.

Behind the curtain of smoke and murk, I slowly made out a figure. Bent over the glimmering hearth was a stock Highlander wearing a shabby old plaid.

"Hello! Anyone at home?" the question seemed more stupid than usual, and I had to repeat it before the man turned round. The face was tired, lined with creases, accentuated by the soot embedded in their furrows. He seemed about 150 years old. They must be hitting the drams pretty hard in this part of the Glen, I thought. The man gazed through me as if I weren't there. Then slowly coming into focus the face took on an expression of total visceral hatred, and muttered something. Whatever he said was unfriendly so I muttered my excuse and left.

Through the soot-laden fog, I spotted a more substantial stone building, the Clachaig Inn. The Clachaig, you remember, was a huge Spartan barn of a place, guaranteed to be as chilly as the top of the Ben, and very character building, with a couple of half-hearted targes, plaids and claymore, tacked on the wall by the landlord as a reminder that this was a historic highland hostelry, and let no Campbell man or can ever darken its threshold. Now it was all dark oak with rafters slung with plastic deer, and faux pine torches on old iron wall brackets, and a neat touch, a choking fog of real smoke, a bit over the top I thought, but the big fireplace where the bar had been was definitely a good idea. All in all it was a masterpiece of tacky Brewery Baroque. And there he was, Rab, easily recognizable by his wooly hair despite it being half-covered by an old blanket, hogging the fire like it was February. He must have been gey cauld the way he was sitting over the flames bent as a miser grasping after every therm of heat. "C'mon, Rab, give another lad some room, and while you're about it how's about getting a pint in?" I tapped him on the shoulder. The head fell back. I was looking into the empty eye sockets of an ancient skull.

The Miraculous Mountain

"Sod this for a game of soldiers!" I told the ice covered rock in front of me. But then why did I bother? The only person remotely within earshot was my second eighty feet below and he didn't give a monkey's as long as we were off the hill before chucking-out time. I was scratching about on a strip of dubious ice smothering a vertical groove two thirds the way up Ben Nevis, a blizzard blowing inside my anorak and night about to fall. A dodgy move lay in wait on iffy snow with throbbing forearms overdosed on lactic acid to the point where I was about to drop off the mountain. The alternatives were proceed and perhaps fall, or stay put and make it a certainty. The lonely ring peg thirty feet below did not inspire confidence. It was rusty. My heart going like a jack -hammer, was flushing my body through with adrenalin.

"C'mon you idle sod, stop posing, and get a bloody move on, or do you want us benighted?" That was the thing with Dudley, he was so there for me. Even without his encouragement, I knew I had to move. "Get up this bit and it's all over." He said in a more wheedling tone. I glanced up and saw a couple of moves past my lonely station the ridge petering out in a series of indeterminate gullies, and outcrops.

What was I doing stuck up here so late, in these crummy conditions? I kept asking myself as I frutched about on tenuous whiskers of ice. As there was nothing I could do about it, the question was academic. But then the bed and breakfast caper hadn't helped for a start .

"Did you say Earl Grey ?"

"No, thankee, Lapsong Souchon with a touch of lemon and a sprinkle of sugar, please." Dudley had to have his little comforts, "Just a sprinkle, mind," and the landlady who had taken a fancy to him went off to fuss. "Just a sprinkle," said she half mocking, half admiring to her husband hovering uselessly on the fringe of the breakfast room. "Such a particular gentleman," She murmured loving every minute of it. With every little fuddy-duddy fastidiousness my stomach churned like a doomsday clock. B & B landladies don't do Alpine starts, and with each passing minute, I could see a bivouac on the Ben looming larger.

"A full Scottish Breakfast, you'll be having?" The diction was precise, *naice*, with none of the explosive glottal stops beloved of the tartan proletariat. And why not, we've paid for it. So we got our money's worth, wading through a multi-course extravaganza of porridge, bacon, eggs, tomatoes, mushrooms, beans, black pudding and the requisite supporting items. What with that, paying the bill, and complimenting our hostess on her Wedgood China, we were late on the Hill.

Now the conditions. I have always been a believer in 'if it don't feel right it isn't.' Today the ambient moisture content was that of a tepid Turkish Bath, and as we turned the corner into the great Allt a' Mhuillin corrie we saw the proof of the pudding.

"Look at it, Dudley. It's a bag of shite."

He looked. The warmish temperature had melted the Ben into a soggy Baked Alaska, with great sickly grey sheets of ice dribbling down into lumps of black sludge, and soggy gobs of the stuff making little splash bombs on the path.

The other two, Dave and Jim, stopped, took stock and waited for us to make up their minds for them. Odd I thought, as all four of us were familiar with the Ben and it's sullen wintry moods. Today it was at its most malevolent, dark dangerous and dismally off-putting, affording a right Scottish Welcome. Was it was the old climber's ploy subtly deferring the decision to us so they wouldn't have to take the rap for any resulting balls-up?

"If you think I've driven all the way from Manchester, just to put my arse down in some bloody Scotch pub..." Neatly put, Dudley. That was that then. Never mind the weather, when you're out on the heather. Dudley had the car and therefore the casting vote. Predicably Dave and Jim nodded solemnly, so on we went bashing our way upwards over execrable wind-slab snow. The others soon sped ahead, and I could hear above the thump of ice-axes on snow which reverberated like an empty cardboard box.

So here we were stuck high on Observatory Ridge, rime covered breeches crackling in the gale, way past the time when sensible lads were piling into the Jacobite, on snow that you wouldn't wish on your worst enemy. In fact the climbing up to this point had been not much more perilous than your average winter excursion, but through my fault we had lingered longer than was good for us. Dudley ascended with dash and elan, strolling up verglassed slabs like Burlington Bertie, while I more timorous mounted the ice as if I were doing a nervous Cha-Cha. If I had been properly assertive this morning the only thing cold would be the pint I was nursing. "Get a move on." This was me talking to myself. "There's bugger all you can do about it now." My forearms had just been recast into rubber, while further down a knee trembler was on the brink of revving up. After a few nervous false starts I managed to howk my boot onto a thinly iced slab, which held me with grudging adhesion. My left axe planted into neve, was tested with a slight tug. It would hold, maybe. The right axe sunk in soft stuff, was pulled gingerly. The result was not reassuring. Meanwhile my right foot was straying inexorably down the slab wrapped in a cellophane layer of broken ice. I had to move very soon. Catching sight of the shards of ice glinting underfoot, I hesitated. Would the axes hold?

Just then. "For Pete's sake get a jildi on, you lazy pillock." I remembered he had been on one of those sensitivity courses. 'OK,' holding my breath I heaved up. Immediately the right axe pulled like it was going through hot butter. The ice under my crampon shattered into a thousand sparklers as my foot shot down the slab. I was off! I jack-knifed backwards through the dark air, thinking, "Christ that piton has to hold me." There came a resounding ping, and the ring peg was whipped out. Jesus Christ! But Dudley'll catch me on his belay. For a nano-second that thought comforted me. Then out of the corner of my eye I saw a grey shape as he was yanked off his stance, and came hurtling down beside me. The information was processed and so quite objectively, I knew I was about to die. Oh well, this is the way it goes. I put my hands in front for protection, thinking why am I bothering, Andy was chopped on Lochnagar in similar circumstances. These thoughts came to me calmly despite my increasing velocity as the ground a thousand feet below came speeding up to meet me.

Whoops! I was jerked to a halt, bouncing up and down at the rope's end like a demented bungy-jumper. Something had grabbed the rope. The Hand of God perhaps or another supernatural entity. It was a bloody miracle, a one in a million chance, for, as far as the eye could see the wall we had dropped over was vertical, without a bump or projection ruffling its surface. The second I came to rest at the end of the rope, serene detachment went out the window, and bloody terror took over. Whatever was holding my lifeline could just as whimsically let go. Shades of Eurydice snatched from the brink of Hades only to be casually dropped back again into the maws of death. "Help!" I bawled birling back and forth through the air. Out of the mist a surprising number of voices shouted back,

"Where are you?"

"Off the side of Observatory Ridge."

"Do you need the rescue?"

"Yes! Yes! For Christ's sake! Yes!"

"OK, don't worry, just hang on."

Easier said than done but one not so immediate problem was taken care of. In the meantime, a ragged fracture, tailor made for a large hex was staring at me from arm's length. Thank You Jesus! I whipped a moac stopper off my rack, stuffed it into the crack, pulled this way and that till it lodged, and clipped in. It would have to do for the time being. Frantically I fumbled through my harness for a bomb proof anchor. There! I found it. A shiny ice peg with the price tag still sticking to it. I hesitated. It had cost me all of nine quid that week, a pretty penny. Scots miserlieness battled briefly with self preservation. What the bollocks am I thinking? It took about a second for me to work my instinctive parsimony through my cerebellum. Casting thrift to the winds, I hammered the piton hard into the crack, tied on, and immediately the tension surged from my body. For the moment I was safe .

A cry came from above. "A-R-E Y-O-U OK?" This was Jim and Dave in chorus. 'Yea, like balls I am,' I thought, but confined myself to shouting, "Yea, but drop me a rope fast, like."

"Will do. Wait a sec till we get a belay." There followed the ring of a hammer bashing a peg in, while I swinging gently in the breeze, had nothing else to do but take stock. As my mitt had fallen off in the fall, my right hand would soon be out of commission. Below me Dudley hanging upside down with the rope caught round his ankle was pirouetting round in neat little circles. "I'm in the shit," he said. Too right, I thought, and there's sod all I can do to help you. Far below the icy terrain of Observatory Gully beckoned uninvitingly. Not much cause for optimism anywhere I looked.

The wind spun me round to face the rock again. The peg I had hammered in so lustily as a lifeline had shattered the frost riven crack, leaving peg and nut clasped together by what was not much more than a mosaic of tottering biscuit crumbs.

"Oh God!" Peering through the gloom at my disintegrating lifeline, I prayed for the first time in my adult life." I promise if I ever get out of this bleeding jam, I'll never mess around with other people's wives, never steal biros from the kids, and look at their mums as bonking fodder. And I'll never ever, never use people, if You will save me, God." I knew that was a major road block to salvation and if I could get it past the front office I could be home and dry. "I'll make my own cups of tea and not blackmail my girl-friend into brewing up," offering up a specific sample of the previous. Promises, promises. I would have promised the Earth if I had it. Only this time I meant to keep them, honest! Fear cleaned out the mind's Augean Stables, purging life's petty squabbles from my system. Even people I cordially hated came up for re-evaluation. Trying not to breathe on the fragile piton, I made a mental note to make a tick list of the above, seek them out and in the unlikely event of them getting over the initial surprise re-befriend them.

Jim called from up above. "Still allright, Gavin?"

"Am I buggery! Send down a bleeding rope, pronto, mate."

"OK, Won't be a minute with the belay." I heard the dull banging of a piton hammer. He sounded calm and deliberate like it was Monday morning and he was back in the classroom, handing out papers to his pupils. Meanwhile was I imagining things or did the peg really twitch in the crack?

"Hurry, for Christ's sake!"

"Don't worry, Gavin." There followed more banging as another peg was bashed home.

"C'mon, Jim!" It came out high pitched, pure counter tenor-who said castrati were extinct? The peg had shifted ever so slightly, but enough to cause me palpitations. If the rope rolled it would pull nut, peg, and me back onto the original flight plan.

"Would it be too much to ask if you could possibly expedite sending down the fucking rope?"

"Just a mo." No exasperation at all, the assured teacher facing a difficult pupil. Another peg sank home. Slowly out of the fog a rope poked and prodded its way down, slithering like an Arctic snake. I tied on and started to breathe. Another rope was dropped, to which I attached two prussik slings. This was tricky as the gloveless hand was as useful as a lump of wood. I began slowly jumaring up the rope, every step giving me grief. Experimenting with prussiks in the comfort of your own home in front of an admiring audience, whose idea of adventure is a stroll to the pub, is a lot different from Saturday Night on the big, bad Ben swinging back and forth on a frozen cable, with snow pouring in at all the surprising gaps in your clothing. At every step, the knot froze and had to be untied with one hand and teeth, all which frigging about was not aided by the blizzard seriously picking up momentum. There's a lot to be said for sticking to the movies on a Saturday Night, I thought taking a last look at Dudley before the mist rolled in. He was sitting on a snowy ledge, a bit forlorn, but not too much the worse for wear.

When I rolled onto the ledge, for no apparent reason Jim said, "You're a great guy, Gavin." No one sober had called me that for a long time, and it was doubly odd coming after my cock up. I was touched.

He tied me on. "What about Dudley?" I asked, for the first time thinking about someone apart from myself.

"Too late. He'll have to stick it out till morning," and he leant over the cliff to pass the bad news on to poor Dudley. No dithering about making that unpleasant decision. I had to admire his powers of leadership. Two weeks ago I had been on an all night bus from Andorra, and thought it the longest night of my life. Now shuffling about on a tiny ledge on the Ben I recalled it's hedonistic luxury with nostalgia. There were other things I was finding out that night. For instance I never believed it possible to fall asleep standing up. It is, but has the serious drawback of getting jerked awake whenever there is a slump onto the belay. Bin bags over our heads protected us from the worst of the blizzard, but the insistent drubbing of mini avalanches on the plastic, kept us chilly.

It was a bitter night, but I didn't care. For some reason I was as full of beans as a kid on Christmas Morning revelling in a euphoria, that would take weeks to shake off. My situation had bucked up enormously from an hour ago with now a sporting chance of coming out of this one alive.

To pass the time, we concocted little divertissements, with the promise of reward, in the shape of a chocolate biscuit. The law of supply and demand inflated this commodity's exchange rate to such an extent that the prize could only be won by telling a successful joke. A gale of hearty laughter was optimistically judged as the standard to be aimed at; a mere chuckle and you would go hungry.

For a while the icy flanks of the Ben were the unlikely setting for Saturday Night Comedy Theatre. Oldies were dredged up from dusty drawers of memory. Stories about vicars at tea parties, vicars drunk in the pulpit, vicars and choirboys, bishops and actresses, bounced from buttress to gully across the crag making it a bad night for prelates all-round. I am here to tell you that not a biscuit crumb was awarded for the first round. No one laughed; not even a titter escaped from that ledge. Each ribtickler was met by stony silence. It wasn't the way we told them, but it seems humour requires a modicum of bodily comfort and warmth for the funny bone to function. Our currency became so devalued we ended up giving the prize to anyone just having a go. By the way the biscuits turned out to be very salty, something you don't notice under normal non dry-mouthed conditions.

Dawn came seeping in grudging and grey, mist blanking out every feature. At cock crow, the buzzing of rotors heralded our rescue. Then the helicopter hoved into sight, circling above the hut, firing off green smoke bombs like it was *Apocalypse Now*. The chopper hung in the sky above us, its rotors gyrating only feet away from the cliff. Out popped our Redeeming Angel in the shape of an RAF corporal at the end of what seemed like a fishing line, hands clasped in front of him as if praying. Here was a joker who could get a real laugh.

We pointed our frozen mitts down the crag, and Dudley was winched up first. Then it was my go. I managed to irritate the boy in blue, bouncing to and fro from the ledge like Peter Pan on a slack wire because cack-handed me couldn't untie my knot, what with one hand a frozen lump and the rest of me not much better.

"Haven't you got a fucking knife?" He shouted unangelically. No a fucking knife was something I had omitted to bring along. Dave sorted out this one, hacking the Gordian Knot apart with his axe, and the next moment I was flying skywards arms clasped ardently round the corporal's neck. When level with the chopper, someone grabbed me by the seat of my pants, threw me into the cabin, -so this is how they do it- and then checked me for damage. The others followed tossed in like potatoes bouncing about in a hopper, and without further ado we were whisked off to Fort William for our brief encounter with media stardom.

Flash-bulbs popped, mikes and cameras thrust in our faces, as we were served up for our fifteen minutes of fame. Jim the real hero of the *Affaire* rendered himself ineligible for celebrity by refusing to play up for the cameras, answering each stupid question in an abrupt, 'How can you ask such a stupid question?' manner. Unsatisfied the battery of cameras, mikes and electronic gizmos swung round to face me. Sensing he was not giving them the goods, I put on my 'I am seriously thinking about this,' act, when they asked me 'what were you thinking about when you were falling?' I pondered, looked straight into the camera's lens and replied gravely that all I could think of were the generations of schoolchildren who would now be deprived of the full riches of their education. On a lighter note I regretted all the exercise books I had failed to mark. I was asked that daft question so many times I began to believe my daft answer. Getting into my stride I described with much gesticulation, the drama on the mountain so that I, the screw-up, emerged as a charismatic TV personality, holding the nation enthralled for all of the two and a half minutes allotted to me, while Jim the real man of the moment found himself relegated to a minor footnote. Funnily enough my mates did not seem to resent me hogging the limelight, so maybe they were all camera shy.

The linesman was wheeled out and we were made to shake hands, no hardship in that, but it made me wonder how many similar gestures are set-ups. I was asked to say something, but I must have given my all in the previous interview for all I could think of to say was "Thanks." He was then asked to say a few words. Oh dear! Here we go. I'll be exposed as an incompetent wally expecting other people to risk their lives. But all he said was, "Next time take a knife." He was a professional after all.

That night we were on every TV channel; after the usual litany of disasters, the up-beat finale to the Sunday night bulletin, so we could all go cheerfully to work on Monday. At school I had the novel experience of being stared at as an interesting phenomenon with an aura, nothing to do with my miraculous escape, but because I had been on the box, and for a moment walked with such deities as Terry Wogan, and Simon Dee.

For the next week we were fodder for the press, receiving all sorts of unwarranted attention, and at its end we were tossed aside, last weeks news, all that was required of us now was to provide wrapping for fish suppers. We had been picked out of obscurity as a freak phenomenon, for during that weekend eight, not so lucky people had died in the Central Highlands and Ben Nevis. Somebody up there had liked us.

The episode had a weird postscript. Instead of being chastened, I went around in a state of intoxication, thinking I was invulnerable, an Achilles without his foot problem. I insulted bigger folk than myself in pubs, put lighted cigarettes in mates' pints, and went barging up to women, who wouldn't have touched me with a barge pole. Fortunately this notion of immortality wore off before they locked me up, although my odd behaviour caused not a few friendships to be put on hold. Nowadays, of course I would have been diagnosed as having an interesting syndrome, and put into therapy, then they just kept me at arm's length in the pub, till I had passed a satisfactory period of probation.

Twenty years on I seldom think of the incident, involving as it does dwelling on the awful consequences if the rope had twitched a millimetre or so to the side. When I do think on it, I ask, why me? Life since has done me few favours, nor have I reciprocated. I have not been set aside for some special destiny. My country has never called me in her hour of need. No cure for cancer has been discovered in my laboratory. I have no cello concertos to my name. I haven't even found a new way to cook chicken.

37

Life goes on. The four of us drifted apart, as is the way of things. An occasional Christmas card and an even more occasional sighting has to do for the camaraderie of the rope. Last summer, I bumped into Jim in the Lakes. An indifferent damp week had terminated in a glorious weekend. We were sitting outside the New Dungeon Gyll enjoying the Lakeland summer evening, contented with our outing on the hill and relishing our pints. He had had a great day, he said, and now seeing me had topped it all off for him. The compliment as unexpected as it was undeserved reminded me of the nice thing he had said when I turned up on his belay ledge. Perhaps, just for that it was all worth it.

I did go back to the Ben, once. Despite my urban *braggadocio* the incident had shattered what little confidence I had on ice, so when confronted with this medium I climbed with timid skittering steps, tentative surges followed by scurrying retreats, and as a consequence had to go back to relearning the basics. After completing my remedial apprenticeship, I sought out a climb suitable for my swan song. We chose Green Gully; nothing would induce me to cross swords with Observatory Ridge again.

Rod and I climbed it late in the season, so fortunately we had plenty daylight. The four major ice pitches were tackled successfully and we arrived below the cornice just as the sun was dropping behind the Ben. I climbed a rope's length on very steep unconsolidated snow. No falling here; Rod had only a fragile ice-axe belay. The cornice overhung by about four feet. I crept up to nestle beneath it like a sparrow under the eaves of a house. Tapping the ice I realised it was so concrete solid that my axe couldn't even make a scratch and it would need a pneumatic drill to break through this lot. My familiar icy companion, fear, seized me. Our position was unenviable, for we were virtually sealed in the gully. No one could help us for by now the plateau would be as deserted as the Sahara. Over to the left I could make out faintly beyond the swirling snow devils, a steep arete where the cornice had collapsed, which just had to be the way out. Reversing the steep unstable snow was something I would rather not linger over. After an anxious half hour I reached the exit, clamped my axes over the edge, and performed a neat Western Roll to end up sprawling on the summit plateau. Beneath us and the icy crusts of the mountains, the whole world was as black as Hell's Night, excepting the great sea lochs, which the echo of the sunset had plunged into molten fingers probing into Scotland's dark heart. We trudged down the hill, crampons making that satisfactory creaking noise, when you know all is well with the snow. The wind cutting across the plateau made us suddenly aware of the cold.

Il Vento, il Vento

You have probably never heard of the Punta di Zocca. But then why should you? It lies on the humble Italian side of the Bregaglia with no star quality neighbors excepting the Badile and the Cengalo, and all you see of them is their boring backsides. There isn't even a decent pub nearby, so no Brits go there, which might make for a good reason to visit.

There is a light-hearted air about the region. The whole range faces into the sun, has few dour Switzers as far as I can tell, and only the merest dribble of steely-jawed Teutons, and there's not a snail's chance a Frog will be there The Italians are more *che sara, sara;* go about their business smiling, selling you ice cream singing snatches of operatic aria while taking your last lire, so that even when they drop stones on you it's hard to take offence.

We stocked up on the usual crusty loaves and cheeses in Massimo, hoisted our packs on our backs, then made our way past woods and streams to the start of the hut walk, past friendly hikers colorfully addressing us in Latin, "Servus! Salve!" all pleasant and relaxed, very different from the frenetic competitiveness of Chamonix. Despite a passage through fine scenery of tumbling waterfalls and huge crags the hut march was as hateful as always. The Allievi Rifugio, our destination, three heavily slogged hours away, is perched like Dracula's castle on the lip of a large boulder strewn cirque ringed by a witch's coven of spiky peaks.

"We are going for the Via Paravicini on the Zocca. Anything we need to know?" The hut guardien, a giant in a hairy red sweater gave us a sour look, snarled, "Fulmine! Fulmine!" pointing to a black spike resembling a wizard's hat, on whose tip a black ball of cloud was twisting, morphing its way through a cornucopia of malevolent shapes, and then waved away any further questions with a grunt before walking off. That was all we were going to get. The chilly Alpine evening made the mountain look menacing and uninviting. We shivered and went inside to our soup and loaves.

Without any hesitation I have to say, that the Via Paravicini is the best route I have ever done in the Alps, better by far than many more glamorous contenders. A short ankle wrenching boulder field places you at the foot of a slim pyramid of brown granite, which allows more graceful climbing than its counterpart in Chamonix. Set in front is two thousand feet of perfect granite, sculpted by a god who loves climbers. There are walls, slabs, intricate knight's move, pitches perfectly pitched at a testing, but never gripping level, the next hold just in the right place, a pocket, a jam, a not intimidating mantelshelf, and blessedly best of all protection placed just within reach. You don't feel molly coddled, but there is an exhilaration with the exposure that is well short of the life threatening, you normally encounter on your voyages into the vertical.

We were climbing well. Nothing could stop us. Here comes the crux, a glorious soaring sky sweeping diedre. I stem up, relaxed and easy, only my twinkling toes are tickling the rock. Where is gravity today? I made a series of delicious, delicate balancy moves, moving upwards without the usual here I go, no I don't style of upward movement, that yo-yo of diminishing returns. It is one of these days of dream climbing, where anything goes, and I wished all the girlfriends I ever had or ever will have could just see me now. But it was just me and Mick, metaphorically patting me on the back after grunting and hauling his ungainly way up, "Fuck Me! That were a fuckin' great lead, youth!" I demur modestly, "It were nowt." Hoping he will mention it in the *Briton's Protection* back home, without being prodded with a free pint.

Pitch after brilliant pitch. Gear placed, runner on, "Bit of Slack!" "Take in for Christ's sake!"

"Up you come. Just do it. It's easy."

"Tight! Make it real bleedin' tight!" Slyly you smile to yourself, self-centeredly pleased that he found it so hard.

In the background the scenery was doing all it could to match the drama on the wall, with assorted peaks, buttresses, turrets and towers, so many storied Camelots, that Disneyland's wildest fantasies could never match. There is more to heaven and earth than are dreamt of in your philosophy, Walt. Enthroned magnificently above all of those, La Disgrazia sat splendid and sublime, its snowy crown, an unravished bride under her shining white veil. Surely she was smiling on us, and there in the opposite direction nestling down in the dell was the emerald shimmering surface of Lake Como. I could just make out the little village of Dongo. Mussolini was murdered there together with his mistress Clara Petacci on just such a day as ours. I push away the thought, but a momentary shiver upsets my Karma. I look closer. On the sheet of blue satin scratched by speedboats tearing across the lake, I imagined Playboys, hair sleeked back and swarthily chested cutting crazy patterns on their water skis, flashing Latin smiles at their thong bottomed beauties broiling on the beach. Kiddies games, as pointless as fish nosing aimlessly in an aquarium. I allowed myself a silent sneer. They would never know that their fashionable frolics contained not an iota of the richness of our experience.

"Watch that bleedin rope! This is fuckin' hard! Why am I carrying your fucking rucksack up this fucking chimney, squeezed like a fucking cork in a fucking bottle!"

Ah. It's back to the real world again. "Ok! Ok! Ok! Keep your flipping wig on!"

It was Mick's turn to lead the only scruffy pitch on the climb, a caterpillar of grass choking an amiably angled crack. Far away to the South East an inky cloud was boiling up like smoke, while I ascended the hairy green road.

"Looks like it's brewing up like shit over there." Mick had also noted it. The advancing cloud from being a speck in the sky was now massing over all the middle distance peaks, pouring through the gaps and passes between the mountains faster than we were climbing.

The last pitch was an old-fashioned zigzag crack on rock reminiscent of Aonach Dubh in Glencoe. Come to think of it maybe it was the damp mist settling on the rock, putting the kybosh on our nonchalant friction climbing that reminded me of home. I mean, for Pete's sake, I had to be sack hauled up the last pitch and my final cheating handhold was a desperate last gasp grab at the summit crucifix. "Cheating. Are we now? Mick was happy, "Great lead, youth!" I wheezed, but I had my fingers crossed behind my back. Lifting my head to sample the summit vista I was hit by a wallop of sleet, frozen rain and snow.

"Let's get the fuck out of here!" Well there was no arguing with that. We were carrying the usual Brits abroad minimal gear, like we were in Sunny Italy. My cagoule had all the rain-resistant properties of blotting paper. Mick's was a little better. If the storm had hit us half way up the climb... No future in dwelling on that. Our walk out gear was far away at the foot of the climb, so with rock boots on we slipped and slithered from rappel station to rappel station. "Careful!" Both of us knew this was the most dangerous moment. Easy rock you could skip down on, now slippery lethal; and us both knackered.

There was a simultaneous flash and crack. I felt my hair standing on end, even under the helmet. "That's the fuckin' *fulmine*, he were on about." We were about halfway down, maybe. You can't really tell. It's always further than you think. Now and then, the mist would swirl away revealing a huge black abyss, which made swinging about at the end of the abseil rope looking for rappel points and landing on slippery ledges fairly intense. The heap of tat attached to the one, or two sorry looking pegs would never pass muster on any outdoor education course. Our nerves were pretty stretched, and that may or may not have had something to do with what came next.

"Listen! Can you hear it?"

"Hear what?"

"It's like fabric, fabric flapping in the wind."

"That's your cagoule, Dick -End."

"No it's not, and listen... Can't you hear crying, a woman crying?" I stopped. Mick was in no mood for para-psychological research.

"Ballocks! Just watch the fuckin' rope!"

He was dead right in his priorities, but I could hear quite distinctly a distressed female voice cutting through the organ pipes of the rock. Once again my mind changed program to something absurdly irrelevant. The woman was having a screaming orgasm. I knew girls that went in for this sort of histrionics. Wow! She must have some lover, some sadistic bastard of a lover by the sound of it.

"What the fuck are you doin'? For fuck's sake! Watch it!" I was about to throw the rope down the cliff without threading it through the junkyard of slings.

"Shit! Sorry!"

"That's all right. Forgiven, but for fuck's sake keep your mind on't job in hand."

"OK point taken." I didn't ask him about the voice now keening in hopeless anguish.

"Look! Look at the way you've got your rope through the descendeur!"

"Oh!"

The rest of the descent went smoothly, if damply. The rope squeezing through the descendeur gushed forth freezing water, which slid down our sleeves via armpits to come to rest forming a puddle at the back of our necks. We collected our trainers and hobbled down the boulder-field, which was much nastier now covered in snow and slush. We slithered hither and thither down the slope to the hut; lucky we didn't break our ankles.

We were on our third bottle of wine, I think, when I remembered about the creepy sound effects. Mick admitted he had heard something peculiar, but hadn't said anything as my absent mindedness was making him nervous. The guardien was as impatient as ever when I asked him about it, "Il vento, il vento." The wind, the wind. He waved his hand dismissively. This was not interesting to him. What was interesting was the large bill we had racked up together. "Il conto, il conto!" He was holding it up close to our noses in case it had passed our attention, his pudgy fingers honing in on the statement of the vintages, clearly taking us for the non-paying Brits who legged it off downhill without as much as a goodbye.

In our club back home, there are two types of bar room pundits. Actually that's putting it mildly, but for now it will suffice. Take Larry for instance, everything accessible to technology is at his fingertips, the Internet, I-pod he's all over it. There I was back in the snug of the Briton's Protection asking him if he had any beta on my story. I could see the words, "Get real!" forming up behind his eyes, before he turned back to his acolytes to tell them about a new device to resurrect fallen leaders. No joy there.

Representing the other category of erudition was Stefan, sitting in lonely state at the opposite end of the bar holding his cigarette like he was an intellectual. He was a walking library of mountaineering history and gossip. Everything in print about climbing he had at his fingertips. So if you were too illiterate to read what Whymper said on his way down from the Matterhorn, just ask Stefan.

I asked him. He assumed a look of exquisite pain, imagine the Delphic Sybil asked by a Persian who was favorite to win at Marathon. "Sorry. You've got me stumped for the moment. Wait till I get home, and I can check. I'll ring you." True to his word he did call, hardly half an hour after drink up time.

"Have I got something? Let's meet tomorrow, and we'll talk." Tomorrow was Saturday. That meant I was lumbered into taking him climbing. The nicest guy to buy you a pint, but on the rock Stefan was no Nijinsky. Well things might be different this weekend, maybe, I thought trying to make optimism triumph over experience.

We did Crow's Nest Crack which as everybody knows is as neat and nice a VS as any to linger over on the odd sunny day in the Coe, but it was September when a warm day can turn freezing whenever the sun goes behind a cloud. He took so long seconding I thought I was turning into the legendary brass monkey. At last, the Kingshouse, and we are settled with our pints and the cigars, which Stefan had thoughtfully bought to celebrate our triumph over the Crow's Nest. "It's an amazing story, a

Princess Di conspiracy theory. The Vatican was in on it, even Camorra hit men." The story, summarized here, took the rest of the night and most of the ride home the next day.

It was a variation on the oldest story in the world. Claudia, the girl in the story had been made pregnant by the son and heir of an Italian automobile manufacturer, and was loudly insisting he marry her to legitimize their offspring, but according to her evil wishers solely to get her hands on the dibs. The boy, Fabrizio said fine, but if she was to be united with him in marriage she should share in his passion for mountain climbing. With the family fortune beckoning, she was neither poor nor honest apparently, she was prepared to take leave of absence from the silks and satins of Milan's fashionistas for a spell in wooly mountain britches. Others said, far from being a heartless gold digger she was but a poor *contadina*, honest, but a hearty embarrassment to a young man of promise and fortune already affianced to a Spanish Bourbon princess, and thus it was necessary she be got rid of.

After an apprenticeship on the crags round Lake Como, Claudia was taken on several Alpine expeditions, and to everyone's surprise, including her own, found she liked the sport and took to it like a squirrel. The plan was for Fabrizio to take her up the Punta Zocca, where in the mists and rocks it would be so easy to have an accident. He made love to her on a handy bivouac ledge, strangling at the moment of coming with her nylon stockings. Tying her up with these was a fetish of his, so she never suspected a thing till the noose tightened. Fabrizio staggered back down into the valley, distraught. She had been killed rappelling when the rope had caught round her neck, and she had fallen. Luckily for Fabrizio the body was never found. Nobody searched for long. It was the time of the murder of Matteotti, which effectively chased the story off the headlines. Some time after this, climbers on the Zocca began hearing the ghost begging for mercy, but there were few willing to look for the sorry lass, with her fondness for pleading during storms when there were prior calls upon the climbers' attention. Further searches in good weather uncovered nothing. Finally a climbing priest performed an act of exorcism, but that too failed to lay the unhappy ghost to rest.

Mick and I went back to the sunny side of the Bregaglia, staying at the Refugio Fiorelli, where a still for juniper poteen added to the general jollity. We did routes on the Sfinge and the Pyramid, not serious, comparable say to longish middle grade routes in the Cuillin but with sunshine added. After all we were on holiday, and we had enough energy to enjoy the nightly party that went on all the season. Every day, it seemed, the same Italian couple popped up to meet us roundabout the first or second pitch, gorgeously appareled like models on an exotic shoot. We could tell they were coming simply by the medley of aftershave and perfume that wafted up towards us. No wonder the man held his nose as they glided past us, climbing impeccably.

"Come tuo Lamborghini!" says the girl laughing, as she overtook us enthusiastically swinging on our runners on the sound principle expounded by Mallory, "Because they are there." The soles of her rock boots were gleaming black rubber, as pristine as if they had just been removed from a Dolce & Gabbana shoebox that morning. Although each foot was neatly placed, the anxiety of the novice, eager to emulate precisely the steps laid down by her master could be detected in her bottom's busily twitching in harmony with the maestro's languid movements. She was in haste; the unforgiving rope like a dog's lead attached to her master made sure of that. But she did at least smile down at us when given a moment's respite, and say, "Grazie!" for the use of our karabiners. That was Carissima, bubbly personality, springy black hair, and big black eyes, who seemed to have taken rather a fancy to me. In the evening she ran about making tea when we came in, all in all making for a pleasant homecoming. Her rope-mate had said nothing to us on the climb, except when he swanned past us, and snorted at our primitive gear. "British engineering," he sneered tugging my badly placed Friend loose. In the Refugio he commandeered the best armchair by the hearth; not resented by the other Italians, I noted, so he must have been a star slumming it for his girlfriend. All his comments were greeted with sycophantic chortles. To us he said, "Hey, Scozzese, where's your doodle sac?" Or, "Let's see what you have under your kilt." Leading to a further outburst of unbounded hilarity by all and sundry with the exception of Carissima, who smiled at us and occasionally filched delicacies for us to help brighten our grim provender.

One evening was spent on story telling, which was dominated by the boy friend. He was your film star Latin Lover, hairily chested, as against aggressively bald on top, tanned like a walnut, and sporting a large medallion that nestled coyly in the curls of his body beard. He spoke five languages fluently, usually all at once. In a word he was mister Charisma and naturally dismissive of us Brits scarcely letting us get a word in edgewise. With various arrogant flicks of fingers and laying on of hands, he demonstrated ownership of Carissima, who in the meantime was sending off flirtatious encouraging signals to yours truly. He had the nonchalant aura of belonging to the rich man's world, she the eager air of a prospective candidate.

By dint of a sustained bout of coughing, a useful spoiling tactic at committee meetings, I managed to get my foot in the door, and wouldn't let go till I finished my story about our ghastly experience on the nearby Zocca, last year. I told the tale in a mixture of Italian and English, which made it more dramatic, all the time hamming it up something awful with spectral shrieks and moans of pain or orgasmic ecstasy, which it was up to the audience to choose. Carissima was drinking it all in delightful adoration. There was a storm outside, and the tilly lamp swaying and flickering in the gloom, aided the atmosphere of the supernatural. I held the company spellbound.

All except Signor Big Gong, who sniggered annoyingly at the best bits. I finished the tale to the applause of all, excepting the aforesaid, who with hardly a pause said, "What was it you said you did?" I hadn't but nevertheless.

"I'm a teacher."

"Of history?"

I nodded, "How did you know?"

"I, let us say, just knew." I didn't say anything sensing checkmate was coming down the route.

"And you didn't know that Matteotti was murdered in 1924, and your route wasn't climbed till 1937?"

"But! But! But! ..."

"Never mind but, but, but. It's an urban legend, Old Boy," At least he wasn't aware that that condescending locution was pathetically dated. "Everybody has heard of somebody who has heard of it, but no one has heard it, because it never happened."

"But the voice, the screams, the crying?"

"Il vento. Il vento, Caro Scozzese."

Carissima looked at me, whether with derision or disappointment uppermost in her eyes, I couldn't tell. Perhaps I have hated someone else as much but not in that moment. By the way I found that wasn't her real name. It was the Italian for 'Darling,' which he called her incessantly in his precious upper class manner.

In the morning, we had a hangover. "Too late to climb. Let's go down." They had gone already. Dutifully we placed a farewell note of intention in the hut book, "Campsite, Massimo." The entry above read, "Roma Traverse--Allievi Refugio--Punta di Zocca, Via Paravicini, Fabrizio/ Claudia."

Green Go!

I went to Mexico in March 95 to get in some altitude training as a prelude to Peru by climbing the volcanoes near the capital. It came as a surprise to me to discover such high peaks were virtually unsung. Still fuming from a recent eruption, Popocatepetl, the most famous of the summits was too angry to receive visitors. Wheezing my way along a neighboring peak I could see puffs of smoke blowing heavenwards like a red-Indian smoke signal from an old time Western. It's slightly heretical to say this, but I didn't miss Popocatepetl, and its slopes of loose cinders. It had all the boredom of perfect form a cone with its top sliced off, Schiehallion writ large. Climbing it two steps up and one step down would be one awful slog. Sisyphus had more fun climbing.

Another surprise was Mexico City. I had expected to find squalor, but not charm, and the girls; they were so pretty I could have been in Dublin's fair city. Walking along the Avenida Reforma exercised my neck muscles. Poverty and opulence went cheek by jowl. Chic and elegantly clad ladies earnestly discussing hairdos and accessories were constantly pestered by Indian beggars, who with few manners and sometimes less limbs should have been out of place on such a refined street, but I didn't realize till later that they were invisible. Outside every bank a posse of police stood

51

silently with sub-machine guns at the ready, waiting on the morning's peso delivery. It was somewhat unsettling going into Dunkin' Donut's and being confronted by a guard with a sawn off shotgun placidly munching his glazed coffee donut trying to make sure his sticky fingers did not mess up his shiny barrel. Robbing banks must be a major Mexican hobby.

Armando, my personal guide, proudly showed me a crumbling fortress in the heart of the city, from whose lofty turrets freedom fighters defied the Yankee aggressors in the Mexican-American War. In the intervals between shot and shell the defenders urged the Americans to return home. With limited English but admirable verbal economy they shouted down to the forest green uniformed soldiers, "Green go!" adding 'gringo' to the lexicon. However according to the etymological dictionary I consulted the root probably comes from Griego meaning Greek, an all-purpose word for foreigner, but I will stick with Armando's more picturesque version.

I did not have long to be engaged in these reflections for soon I was whisked up to the base camp for Malinche, a fourteen thousand foot midget volcano, considered a suitable height for acclimatization. I thought wistfully of the good old days in the Alps when we would spend the first week under ten thousand feet before poking our nose into the double digits, and promptly woke up with a raging headache and a wheezy chest. Hector, the head honcho guide said it was par for the course, and I would feel better as we climbed higher. As there was no alternative, I decided to believe him, and so we set off up through the woods, his flamenco dancing girlfriend racing in front. These Mexicans had a sense of humor like the Scots, biting and merciless to their friends. You had to get up early in the morning to keep your reputation intact. Another nostalgic feature was the sense of inferiority they had towards the great English-speaking nation on their doorstep, and their love of showing how they sorted them out, with their unhistorical method of exaggerating the insignificant and minimizing reality. Gringos and Bannockburn. But what really made me feel at home was the volume of swearing. If any sentence was not punctuated by at least four seriously nasty profanities it could be written off as bland. Swearing was the chili sauce that flavored their conversations. It was refreshing being back where you didn't have to watch your tongue all the time. Hector liked the Scots. He had met many on his expeditions and found them to all as hard as nails. This didn't come as good news to me who is not of the same caliber of metal, and felt pressured not to let the side down.

I learnt all these things as we trekked up our mountain. Malinche was an Indian girl, who became the mistress of Cortez and helped to win over the Aztecs. From being a heroine who helped mold the Mexican character she is now looked on as a base traitor to all things indigenous. Fashion is everything in history and we may look for her reputation to be restored in the next recycling of the past. At the moment anyone who likes Coca-Cola in Mexico can be accused of being a Malinche- a dangerous jibe.

But for the present Malinche was like climbing Arthur's Seat when you have a severe case of flu. Would you climb Mont Blanc the day after arriving at Chamonix? I swore fruitily in my newly acquired vocabulary and got a look of total amazement from Hector and a chuckle from a pleasant senorita standing by. Otherwise I don't remember a view. Hector wished us well. He was off to Cho-Oyu the next day. He thought my endeavor would be successful. Had my bad language secretly impressed him? I never found out, but apparently I was a passable Scot.

If first impressions count, I learnt a lot about Mexico and Mexicans in those ten days. The stereotypes of handlebar moustaches somnolent under sombreros they were not. The ones I came across were lively, educated and full of fun with an interest in the world beyond their parish, altogether lacking the creaking inner psyche of their neighbors to the north and the melancholia that comes with having a surfeit of possessions.

One incident made an impression. Driving through a village that could have featured in a spaghetti western we almost scattered a kids football game kicking around a battered beach ball. The goals were heaps of garbage strategically posted, and the mud brick wall of a pueblo. All around was Third World poverty, but none of that mattered, the kids were having the time of their life. They were the happiest children I had seen anywhere.

We drove on into the night to meet up with one of the great characters of the Mexican peak adventures. I was surprised when Armando simply asked for Jorge, our host for the next night or two, by name in the street. To find Jorge's address we just asked the first person we met on the street, not a method that stood good chance of working in Manchester, or Glasgow, but then Mexicans still have a sense of community that we only find in telly soaps. Jorge is a character, ex-mayor, businessman and general all round good lad. His first response on meeting you is to go for the goolie area, slap you on the back and color the air blue with a print out of your intellect, lack of, parentage, lack of and sexual proclivities surfeit of. This happened to Armando, who was a friend. Not having been introduced, I was received slightly more formally. He is as they say not for the faint-hearted, and of course climbers round the world adore him. Postcards from the late and great from every continent testified to that. Of more general interest the final showdown in Butch Cassidy and the Sundance Kid was filmed from his doorstep. Check it out. There is no mistaking Pico de Orizaba looking down on the square where the two buddies met their end.

Jorge's job apart from feeling us up and feeding us with re-fried beans was to transport us to the base of Pico de Orizaba, the highest mountain in Mexico and the third highest in the North Americas. This was somewhat harder than it sounds. At one point his sons had to get out of the wagon and build the road ahead, the local authorities being more than usually neglectful. While this was happening the heat inside the lorry rose to 100degrees, and Jorge was playfully mauling Armando's thighs and encouraging him to be less shy by calling him all sorts of pervert. Subtlety never wore a sombrero.

The shack where we spent the night reminded me of the huts when I first started climbing, the Dray in Glencoe, Wall End Barn at Langdale, and Tyr Pwyder above the Pass, plenty of draughts, the scampering of mice during the restful hours and the fragrance of forgotten milk and ancient PAs. I woke up to a splitting headache. We spent the day kicking our heels, exchanging bullshit with other climbers and in the evening climbed a thousand feet to establish a campsite at 15000ft on the bottom edge of an ice slope. I awoke to the pleasant surprise of no headache and watched the torches of two Norwegian girls lightly skipping up the slopes in front of us. In the dark we mounted the curiously kipper shaped ice field by following the line of its backbone.

At sixteen thousand we stopped as a bleached sunrise peered timidly at first, then gaining confidence began trundling heavily over a landscape of dirty rocks. The hardest day in my life had begun. I kept trying to zigzag to de-escalate the ferocity of the slope, but Armando kept tugging at my rope as if I was a stroppy dog stopping to pish on every bush. Like plunging into a lake and finding the other shore keeps getting further away this slope got even more unrelenting with every upward stride. There was one technical bit that required a half-hearted rope round ice-axe belay and sinking of mitts onto the ice, which was a relief as it gave something else to think about. "Tienes cojones," Armando kept encouraging me as I wheezed on up to the final slopes onto the jagged edge of the cone. Cloud boiled up to spoil the view. I stumbled on up a dull gray pile of shale to collapse on the summit, 1500 ft short of the magical 20,000 ender. Another metaphor for life? Armando took out his cell-phone to call his girl friend. I was invited to call my wife at work. I pretended not to know the code; too shagged out to speak and wasn't up to dealing with the secretary, who saw her job as designed to keep all callers at bay.

On the way down the fish shaped ice field was gushing with water. Everything was grey slushy mud. I fell on my backside several times getting my nice new gear dirty. Maybe I wasn't concentrating for I was thinking that one lesson learnt from this first exposure to serious altitude, was that like every one else who had put their time in building up a solid portfolio of experience before venturing higher, I was inclined to smirk at the over compensated over-achiever buying their way up Everest with their crampons on the wrong feet. There was a bit more to it than just laying out 65 big ones.

After a rest we camped at about twelve thousand feet on the sandy slopes of Iztaccihuatl, which is Aztec for the sleeping princess. Dormant or not, strange are the ways of the gods in making our innermost dreams come true. I was about to mount a princess, from her knees to her knockers. As it was about 1,500 ft shorter than Orizaba I thought I would find it a bit easier. Little did I realize that in the best traditions of Arthurian Romance, to win her royal highness I would have to give it my all. On the path up a predawn chorus of coyotes greeted us. Armando warned me, "Don't step on any rattlesnakes," adding, "You may not die, only suffer horribly." Was what you may call a cheery after thought. By the time we reached the royal knees the first cold purple rays of the sun charged the sky. Slowly I maneuvered myself up towards the thighs. I would like to say with mounting excitement but that would be a fib. The entire erogenous zone was a slithery gravel slope like fighting one's way up a down escalator. Popocatepetl was like this the whole way I was told. Exit Popocatepetl from my list of dreams and desires. Still the colors were nice and at least the view changed as we were going up a ridge. At last, and I can't resist saying this, we breasted the summit. The nipple, a massive cairn of stones set over rotting ice and slush was covered with old bottles and empty sardine cans. Thus was the Aztec Goddess honored.

I have to say the volcanoes of Mexico are pretty dull fare. Aesthetically the whole business was on a par with climbing Mount Piccadilly near Kingsbury in Warwickshire, which took less time, much less pain and rewards its conqueror with a view not obscured by cloud. The excitement was provided by the question of whether I could actually get up High Hills. The highlights of the trip were meeting Mexicans, whom I found jolly and without the bloated pretensions of their Northerly neighbors, and surviving cultural experiences such as eating *mole*, a disgusting mixture of chocolate, chicken and something very hot. Does all the methane digestively produced weaken the ozone layer over Mexico City, I wondered in a rare moment of scientific interest. The best views were not in the mountains, but ogling at the whores on the Reforma, who returned my gaze without any curiosity whatsoever.

On my last day I visited the Aztec pyramids near Mexico City in the company of a guide, who doubled as a bit actor in various movies including Romancing the Stone. He provided a fund of stories, and was charming to us, but I noted he swore like a trooper with his mates. This much I had learned of Mexican *mores*. I made the mistake of speaking to one of the hawkers selling trinkets. Taken as a serious customer, I became a honey pot, dolls, fetishes, little china ornaments were thrust in my face. They wouldn't let me go, tugging at my arm and giving me serious in the face pestering. Sound of wind and limb I turned on a nifty little sprint to elude them. With my newfound fitness I was able to run up the nearest pyramid, leaving them arguing about the lost spoils in the dusty arena. So at least the trip was good for something.

Climbing by Visa

How a guide introduces himself. "Hi! My name's Roke. I'm famous. You must have heard of me?" Pause. "Read about me?"

"No."

"That's fine, Gav. May I call you Gav?"

"No."

"Well that's OK, Gav, being so famous I get fed up with all my groupies following me about back home."

"I promise you'll have no problems there with me, Roke."

Actually I did have a lot of problems following him about because he kept on getting lost on the trail, when wandering through Indian pueblos and over the not very forgiving glaciers. This is not a high recommendation for a guide. But these little discoveries were treats in store for me. Fortunately Stu the other guide did not suffer from unrequited egoism, and so some sensible equilibrium was maintained.

Lima, the capital of Peru, has all the charm of Belfast on a rainy day. Notices on government buildings advised us not to stop or we would be shot at. A vicious civil war had just ended. My memories of it are rubbish everywhere, people living in abandoned cars and three- legged dogs trotting down the streets, not a tourist trap.

Two days walking up an old Inca path took us to base camp. On the way up we passed muleteers lurking in caves, possibly brigands, who considered us not worth robbing. Their womenfolk with their stovepipe hats and wide multi-colored woolen skirts could be taken for the Welsh in traditional fancy garb on their way to a jolly Eisteddfford, but for the babes slung in picnic bags on their backs and of course their dark reddish brown color. Despite all the talk of the "Shining Path," I always felt the natives were friendly.

Surrounded by Alpamayo, Chitaraju and nameless other peaks, base camp was stupendously situated. During the night I surfaced from sleep in a panic gasping for air, my lungs heaving like a dysfunctional bellows. So this was Cheyne-Stokes breathing. It was unpleasant and made me want to pee at the same time. We hiked up to 17,000 ft. Roke, the others' guide had left with his Mormon clients two hours after us just to make a point and caught us up on the moraine two thousand feet above camp, bragging about the performance of his athletic charges, who were really "kicking back." I sat in surly silence putting on my crampons. Just contemplating the pace these 30 some-thinger Mormons were going knackered me, and left me wondering whether I would make it at all higher up, or as they say in the clergy I had my doubts. When the next day later both of them went down with acute mountain sickness, I said to myself, not without a soupcon of malice, the Lord works in mysterious ways.

The last few hundred feet up to the ridge over steep ice, past a landscape of icy penitentes, standing like frozen wigwams, would at Alpine altitudes have been enjoyable, but here were a constant agony of sucking in of thin air. A pitch of loose crunchy snow stands out as a bad moment, where double the effort gained less than half the progress expected, while trying to forget about the awful prospect of the whole slope slithering away, and thrusting us back down into the valley. As we came over the top onto the ridge the wind whipped through our double jackets, bringing in black malignant clouds. There were several tents set up there, grey against the snow, and dusted with spindrift; all the inhabitants hunkered down in their pits. My spirits never high drooped further at the prospect of camping at this dreary spot. The turds dotted around the tents like brown posies did little to enhance the glittering prospect. At this juncture the tension between our two leaders broke out into an unedifying quarrel over where to stash the gear we had humped.

Eventually a brief truce restored harmony, and we dropped down to camp in a basin facing the classic side of Alpamayo, with the mountain revealing itself in all its wide-skirted glory. Our route, the Via Ferrari, sliced its way between two icy flutings going dead up the middle like a zip-fastener. And there we camped in a setting of unparalleled magnificence, ringed around by a crown of wild, icy towers, a reward for what I do not know, but a treasure chest for the eyes that for at least once in a lifetime all mountaineers deserve. That night for no reason at all I dreamt my way through all the Faulty Tower re-runs, and woke up a drowning man gasping for air.

Three o'clock saw me stumbling around nervously trying to find vital odds and sods in the dark. At least I got my gaiters and crampons on the right way round. The scenery as we crunched our way slowly up and around the seracs in the blackness of the night was incomparable. Splendid jagged white giants sprouted from the glacier to stand against a stark black sky, studded with a confusion of unknown constellations, only the Southern Cross being recognizable. We crossed the first bergschrund, which was a very steep snow slope and plowed over a band of deep powder. The second bergschrund was an almost vertical ice-pitch that needed two ice screws for protection. It reminded me of the first pitch on S.C. Gully in Glencoe. These few hard moves gutted me, and not for the last time I wondered if I had anything more to give.

I stepped over the edge and onto a long steep gully of pure neve that ran all the way up to the summit. Every 160feet belay-stakes, as safe as concrete bollards, were hammered deep into the snow. With somebody else doing the leading there was no feeling of danger or fear of falling only the relentless grind against the altitude and the gulping in of air as I stood sentinel on the stances. The night evolved into a gorgeous cloudless day. Unknown mountains stood in file after file till they faded into the limitless blue of the sky. The only marker of our progress was a huge basilisk of stone lodged halfway up on the gully flank. Beyond it the snow turned to unrelenting water ice and my ridiculously named Rambo crampons began to prove themselves clutching the ice in their steely Stallone grip. For the last couple of pitches the gully steepened violently, giving us an ice wall that would be respectable in Glencoe.

My crampons and tools bit into the ice famously. Just short of the top I was spent. I lay my head down in a handy hole and wheezed. Stu tapped me on the helmet with a frosty mitt as if he were taking a spoon to a boiled egg. "Come on up!" The summit ridge I mounted was no wider than a saddle. There was no view. One leg was hooked over the boiling clouds, twenty thousand feet below were the steaming jungles of the Amazon; the other straddled the ice wall that backed onto our camp.

Never was a peak more hardly won so easily forsaken. Clipping on to the stakes we rappelled pitch after pitch back down to the bergschrund from where a short trot took us back to camp, where the others saluted us with a mitten muffled handclap.

It was at this point that Joe 'The Void' Simpson came over the ridge and slowly began descending to the camp. I racked my brain thinking of something momentous to say for future anecdotes in the pub. After all I was with Americans; I dressed like one. Most of all I had lost that furtive thieving look that distinguishes the British climber abroad. To all intents and purposes I was a Yank. Just as he passed I got it, "Hey up then, mate."...

He turned to me wearily, "Sorry, mate, too f..... knackered to speak." I've dined out on that exchange many times. .

For a while I wondered with all the famous people here, if I hung around long enough, might I too become famous? But then I thought if it involved a near death experience like Joe's or being a prat like Roke maybe mediocrity is just fine for me.

....

The path from Muchos to Huascaran base camp was like something out of Beatrix Potter. Trees recognisable from an English country garden were strewn amidst botanically interesting wild flowers. We camped amidst a babel of tongues. All the representatives of the European Union were settling down to a very English Afternoon Tea, surrounded by the impoverished Indios saying not much, but doing everything, and when afterwards they were sitting in their blankets shivering while we lorded it around in warm clothes in a warm mess tent, I felt a prick of conscience, but did nothing. Next day was different. We said goodbye to the colorful flora, and entered the grimmer greyer world of ice and stone. A long trek up an unlovely moraine took us onto a furnace of a glacier. As usual a plantation of jobbies marked our cold exposed campsite. Roke excelled himself by first giving me a lecture on not letting the side down by my slowness, then turning up late after losing the way. The two leaders had another little tiff that simmered on and off for the remainder of the expedition. Because of the cold, sleep was out of the question that night. I could only keep tossing and turning to find the least frigid position. It was another in the long list of my most miserable nights on the hill.

The main event for the next day was the ascendeur pitch. In order to save weight carrying an extra tool, we had to jumar our way up the steep concave wall of ice. I thought it hellishly strenuous and ended up being roped to Roke, who now got a chance to monitor my performance at first hand. "You're not going to make it," he said encouragingly, whenever I tried to pause for a breather. Then "Faster," he urged as we trailed through a collapsed serac zone.

"Can't we stop for lunch?" I suggested, the wilted fragment of pop-tart, that had been breakfast being hardly sufficient for a growing lad like me. "No, too dangerous," he said indicating as a stopping place a huge serac tucked under the col. "There's your lunch stop."

"But that's the camp." I had espied all the brownies spattered indifferently on the snow. "No," he said firmly. It's much too near. What makes you think that it is?"

"I read it in the guide book in Huarez."

"Oh!"

It turned out I was right but that did not make me feel any better as I staggered about trying not to stab the diverse inhabitants of the tent city with my wayward crampons. Roke once again provided encouragement. "Anyway, you're too slow. We took five hours. This section should only have taken two hours."

"But that's the time given in the guide books."

"What?"

"Five hours."

"You sure?"

"Yes"

He looked at me incredulously and then went sheepish. What a winner he was. I got into my sleeping bag, after dining sumptuously on a spoonful of pasta. At this altitude I had zero appetite.

And there was Marcos at the door of the tent, doing his imitation of the Admirable Crichton hand extended with cup of steaming hot tea. When the fur was flying amongst the high heid yins, he was always imperturbable, unflappable and cheerful. This was a morning so cold my water bottles were frozen solid within the tent. The temperature never seemed to affect him and his fellow Indios, this despite the fact they were dressed in old street clothes instead of the extortionately expensive warm, wind proof, snow proof garb we wore. Outside a blizzard was blowing insistently. No pictures today. The ascent itself was one unrelenting trudge, like doing a perpetual treadmill with snow being blown down inside my cagoule from neck to boot. Near the top the murderous slope flattened out somewhat and we were in a lung-bursting version of the Cairngorms. We reached the top. Two Chileans popped up out of nowhere, hugged us warmly, then instantly disappeared back into misty oblivion like spear-carriers in a Shakespeare Play. I had reached the utmost summit of my life. I had suffered grievously and paid steeply in the pursuit of attaining it. This was a moment to pause, reflect on the inner meaning of life, and heartily wish Roke could eat a hedgehog, but all that passed through my mind was. "No more going up."...

Pizarro's Revenge

" We shall be Scholars and Brothers, nay Brothers in Arms in the quest for-how you say it-…for the Great Truth." He took his hand off my knee long enough to point at his disciple, me. The master plan was still simmering.

"Geography, geology the cartography of the Selva we will study. The history of the ruins in their context, social, anthropological and archeological, shall be examined. Musicology, seismology and climatology will we muse over as we ramble through the ruins, amble over the Andes…" My guide and self appointed mentor stopped in mid stride; his muse expired: the bottle stopper glasses were still hotly glinting in the after burn of his exaltation. I wasn't going to help him out. Miguel's itinerary for the intellect, wasn't my cup of tea.

"Well maybe."

"We shall walk through these enchanted Highlands, sniffing the flora, following the flight of the *pajara grande, si el condor.*" Suddenly he was all business, "Manana eight o'clock sharp, Hotel lounge. No buggering about, see!" The finger was again upraised, this time accusingly. The locution from both ends of the verbal spectrum had me impressed; another notch in the belt of my renaissance man, mountain-guide.

The grandfather clock struck eight, and I was on parade, spruced up in boots, togs and hiking poles with price tags still attached, but no Miguel. Sitting opposite was my cook and her husband. In the long silence we tried not to stare at each other. The cook smiled hesitantly, and then all three of us began shuffling and fidgeting as people do meeting for the first time, without even a common language to break the ice.

The husband stirred, murmuring something in rapid Spanish. I gathered it was up to us to go and drag our leader out of bed. We reached his house after a short journey through earthen streets to Cuzco's main barrio, just in time to witness a poignant farewell.

The door opened. Miguel rocketed out to smack the ground yards from the door, swiftly followed by a fusillade of rucksack and boots, which hit him right in the center of his upturned rear. Whoever was doing the eviction had had plenty target practice. He gave a sheepish grin, not impressing anyone that he was in charge of events. A few high spoken words, probably untranslatable followed, a door was slammed; sweet adieux were over; we were ready for the off.

"She forgot I was doing the Inca Trail." Ah! The old climber's body swerve. Not telling the wife that he was off to the hill, till the car was at the door. We've all done it. Miguel's only mistake was to try it on a more formidable significant other than the average. The two unmistakable shiners he sported clarified, if that was necessary, her point of view. Unabashed he launched into a self-serving encomium extolling the honorable estate of matrimony, and his own nuptial set-up in particular.

Probably pretty well used this sort of treatment by now; he quickly recovered his equilibrium sufficiently to allow another glimpse into his multifaceted personality. This was Miguel the Marxist. "I am a *hombre* of the people, *pobre*. My wife *pobre, mios chicos pobre, como nuestros.*" His comradely gesture to include the others was not extended to me. I was not left for long to wonder why. "We live in a poor country *sin futuro* for our *chicos*; not fat, rich capitalist like you." The odd mix of Spanish and English he came up with drew some of the sting of his revolutionary rhetoric, which I had a hunch was all posing anyway. Well it was the first day of the trip, I thought; better let this wash over me.

"That watch, we *pobres* slave for a year and not able to buy." This was an Avocet altimeter, my solitary luxury and had cost me a very pretty penny. Now was only its third outing. Should I explain this? Not much point as he had broadened his target area. "You Gringos come to our country and expect to be treated as *conquistadores*."

"But I'm Scottish not American. Scotland is a poor country." A bit of a lie in comparison to Peru but anyway it was swept away in another relentless torrent of rhetoric. "Your boots, brand new." True. This was to be their maiden voyage, but as they had only cost me $30 at Target were hardly a sample of fat cat purchasing power. I tried to tell him this but was dismissed. "Your jacket, your back pack, all made from the sweat of *campesinos*" He was warming up to accuse me of accompanying Pizarro on his raid on Cuzco's Inca Treasure, when he suddenly swerved onto a different tack, as another feature of our renaissance man emerged, Miguel the avaricious bastard.

"When we finish trip, you give me them." Says he pointing at my offensively bourgeois boots. "Sorry Miguel you're out of luck there. I've booked them to take me on a tour of the Hocking Hills after this. Love to do it otherwise."

"When you finish, you mail them to me. I like the watch. As I am very good guide, you give me as *regalo*." I decided to take an interest in the llamas munching by the side of the road.

That night we camped by the ruins of an Incan Fortress at Ollantaytambo, a way station for the imperial mail network, that stretched over an empire, three times the size of Rome, where tally sticks carried by the runners were used in lieu of writing. Like Shelley's Ozymandias it gave food for thought about how transitory were the works of Man. I now had a retinue of two cooks, two porters as well as my leader/ guide. As an orienteering exercise the Inca Trail is less strenuous than the Penine Way, which gave Miguel plenty time to stroll about with me discoursing on the many topics of which he was the master. His lectures on the Glory that was Inca were encyclopedic, and well worth hearing. I can't recall a word of them, which was my own fault, in launching a petty guerilla action, acting up like an obtuse school kid.

After the archeological seminar we sauntered back to the dining tent, erected by our busy porters. The meals were pretty fair, I have to say; no beer but plenty of tea replenished as soon as you stuck your mug out. As an officer and gentleman, Miguel dined with me at the high table entertaining me with his learned converse; the others had to make do with squatting round the fringes of the groundsheet, keeping the evening draughts away. He was providing an interesting variant on Marxism orthodoxy, or maybe he had read Animal Farm.

All these petty niggles evaporated next day when we emerged onto the ridge-top from camp to see a view to make a saint gasp, the green canopy of the Selva topped by the dazzling white of the Andean mountain chain. I wandered along the stony road in a glorious aesthetic daze, as peak upon stupendous peak reared up as backdrops to the relics of the Inca Empire.

One mountain emerged even more spectacular than the rest. "What's that?" I said. "Salcantay." I had been looking forward for years to seeing this magnificent mountain, reputedly the sacred home of the Inca Gods, so this was a magic moment. At the next corner another higher peak hoved into view. "And this?"

"Salcantay." The road wound its serpentine way along the contours of the hill, amidst ancient forts and way stations, and each new viewpoint revealed more mountains always more splendid than those before, all named 'Salcantay.' I counted five. Miguel was quite unabashed by the mountain having multiplied.

Uninterrupted files of Indians bearing huge shapeless bundles of impedimenta jogged past, laughing, joking and smoking without pausing for breath. Clad in old jeans and torn at the elbow discarded sweaters they seemed a lot happier than the designer clad trekkers making heavy weather of the hike. Unbelievably there were wayside pubs on the trail, advertised by a sprig of heather and a clump of red plastic stuck on the end of a broomstick, where the porters refreshed themselves with jugs of cloudy beer, an excellent arrangement I thought, so I sampled a pint and for approximately 25cents got gloriously drunk, with a swingeing hangover to match. But my willingness to absorb the native culture brought its own reward. That afternoon I rose in Miguel's estimation.

That evening, Miguel's hasty departure began to tell.

"Gabin, it's cold tonight.""Yes?"

He shivered outside my tent to make sure I was with the plot. I was lying snug and warm in my pit to make the contrast more poignant. "I leave in a hurry. I have no jacket to keep out cold." His teeth were really chattering; gone was the expansive bon viveur of the afternoon's refreshment stop. I had a spare cagoule, which I handed to him. "*Muchas, muchas gracias, Senor Gabin.*"

"*De nada.*" I grunted not entirely thrilled.

The next morning I peeled back the tent flaps, to find the hero of the *campesinos* peering into my boudoir, blowing heartily into his clenched fists."Gabin, my hands they are cold." Miguel's was gloveless. I handed him my spare pair. We breakfasted in silence; I in irritation, Miguel gazing into his tea mug, plotting to regain the initiative.

This he did by stopping at every ruin and explained in English of Dickensian turgidity its significance. I counter-attacked by asking him to repeat the spiel in Spanish- both of us were eager to improve our linguistic skills- which he would only do if I gave him a synopsis in that language, which he then deemed unsatisfactory. From there on an undeclared state of war existed between Miguel and me.

We were on the last lap. I wanted to climb a nearby knoll to savour the vista, which encompassed the snowy Andes, the Amazonian Selva, and the first glimpse of Machu Picchu. Miguel was too lazy for this treat and at every undulation he flopped down pretending he had found the best lookout, but I was relentless and made him go the extra step. When I finally stopped atop a sunny spot, I pulled out a tube of very strong sun crème for my Gringo pallor.

"Gabin,...." I didn't wait for the rest, just handed him the crème. He squeezed out a generous splurge and gave back the nigh on empty tube. Miguel had no duties except keeping me entertained, so he had a license to bore me full time. Fortunately the program advertised on the first day, failed to materialize, but I was suffering from a surfeit of archaeology, about which I have to admit, he was exceptionally well informed and occasionally interesting.

That night when I crawled into bed, I realized I was suffering from "Expedition Rage," where every little tic, or mannerism of your best friend pushes you towards homicide, liable to be triggered by an inordinate snuffle, sign-posting every sentence with 'Actually,' or any other sociopathic habit. We have all known long-standing friendships rent asunder by a sneeze carelessly extinguished on a sleeve. In spite of the pre-walk rhetoric, Miguel and I never bonded, and now I had had it with his constant scrounging and evasion of anything that looked like responsibility. Tonight the gods were going to place the means of revenge into my hands in generous measure.

There is a seamless ritual attached to retiring at night. First of all one drains one's bladder, while searching the stars like Keats. "Oh! Look! A comet, a shooting star!" You cry delightedly as your kidneys are flushed out in one last ecstatic gush. This is best done at least five paces from your own tent, and a sight further from others' tents if you don't want yours to collapse in the night. In high mountains such as the Andes the condensation from your breath freezes inside the tent, leaving a sugar coating on the roof. Trying to get out without shaking the tent is impossible and the inevitable uninviting price of a pee is a shower of icy chips down the back of your neck. An obvious strategy to circumvent the problem is the Pee bottle. When the bottle is filled which it will do rapidly, the contents can safely be poured outside the tent without hazarding an exit. I always take two bottles; the other is filled with water to assuage midnight thirsts, making sure which one is placed where.

Promptly at dawn the next day the inevitable bottle top glasses accompanied by the ingratiating grin, popped up in front of my tent. "Gabin," He nodded to my water bottles. We had it down to code now. My conscience briefly fought with my nasty side and lost. The yellow tinted bottle, fortunately empty, was handed out.

I made sure I was there for the tasting. Filling the bottle from the stream, he lifted it slowly to his lips savoring the anticipated joy of drinking pure clean mountain. His expression registered puzzlement, then a flickering facial squirm and finally brightened with dawning realization- he had previously helped himself to a few sly nips of my Famous Grouse- "I think you have added a little something to this," wagging his finger roguishly at me, "To give flavor." He smiled as if he was in on the joke. "I think you make Scotch Water." He never spoke a truer word.

Later, when I had the leisure to ponder on my action, I felt slightly guilty; maybe my reprisal was yet another neo-imperialist European outrage inflicted on the Third World. Whether I should feel bad about it I leave it to the reader to decide.

Tales of a Hillman

By Moira Fiorelli

I wanted to forget all about the An Tealleach affair, and so called my old friend Algy. He was sensitive enough to see that I needed bringing out of myself, and suggested an immediate rendezvous. The thought of meeting the eccentric Scottish nationalist cum mountain memorialist, Algernon MacVitie MacBeth was an immediate tonic and I set out for his flat with a newfound spring in my stride. The doorbell rang with a reassuringly resounding chime. What would it be like inside, I wondered. Would there be a mock up of a baronial hall in Marchmont with stags' heads targes and tartans, affixed by crossed claymores? As Algy helped me off with my coat, I realized that once again my imagination had outstripped reality. Now finding myself in a tastefully decorated modern flat I had to assume that the traces of a Habitat hand at work belonged to the previous owner. On his lounge wall was a print by Paul Klee flanked by what looked suspiciously looked like a Mondrian. The music, that slithered round the walls, originating from a bang up to date stereo system, was unambiguously twentieth century. Was he like most of the people I had dealings with also a charlatan? My expression must have betrayed my thoughts for he said, "Sometimes, Moira, I need to rest from my mission."

Behind his head his clan emblem was surmounted on a sombre strip of MacBeth tartan while beside it was another crest depicting a raven about to take flight from the battlements of a castle. Inscribed on a scroll beneath the motto, "Cras, Cras, Cras." The raven's croak, "Tomorrow and Tomorrow and Tomorrow."

"Suetonius or Shakespeare?"

"Both – perhaps," he answered Sphinx-like passing me a plate of enigmatic buns.

Out of the corner of my eye I could see a coffee table loaded with three plates one of which was piled high with Nairn Tea scones already smothered with Highland Croft Butter. Behind this mound was a jar of Thistle honey.

"Honey on these scones? Isn't that just a teeny bit too much?" said I with mouth full already, ravenously bad mannered.

"When in need, yield to greed." It was sound advice and I tucked in to this delicious over indulgence. My host could tell that I needed taking out of my self. After our coffee table feast he repaired to his story telling armchair and with pipe, puffing away like a jolly steam engine and glass of whisky to hand, he proceeded to entertain me.

My troubles were soon forgotten as I listened enthralled to the stories of Algy's peregrinations. Years later, I realized I had been very privileged that evening. I had had played out in front of me the very adventures that were to form the basis of the tales eagerly awaited by the armchair ramblers of Scotland. In my more cynical moments, which are not really part of my nature - I tend to the credulous - I wondered if Algy was not using me as a test-market. Was he practicing on me, polishing up his anecdotes prior to publication? I assumed that even the great Homer must have employed a similar tryout before releasing the tales of the brave but bone-headed Achilles and the sly Odysseus into the great halls of the ox-eating heroes. I noticed that at the points where I laughed or reacted suitably, these little stories appeared in print verbatim, even to the point of including those little nonsense words that we use to carry the story along, but would jib at putting on the printed page. For instance when describing one of those beautiful sunsets, which are often the reward for those who travel in the hills of the North West, he would say, "By Jove, Moira, it was prodigious!" This would appear in print as, "It was by Jove, a prodigious sunset." I looked in vain for my name under the acknowledgements. Now I don't mean to be a pedant or a bore, but aren't people going to ask questions? Such as "Please explain what exactly is a prodigious sunset. I have been going to Glencoe for my holidays for years and have never seen one." You can get away with anything in speech. In my experience people are not listening, only waiting for you to take a breather so they can get an oar in.

His little pen portraits of the people who inhabited the Highlands were extremely diverting. There was the incident of the mad shepherd who threatened to set his dogs on Algy, if he did not get off his land forthwith. This, he indicated with a wild sweep of his arms, seemed to encompass the whole of Scotland North of the Moray Firth. With great courage Algy stood on his rights and his ground, "I told him ever since the days of Bruce and Wallace, Scotland had been a free country, the very word trespass had an alien English ring. My knees were knocking under my kilt. I can tell you, Moira, it was lucky I had my extra long Victorian one on." These ferocious beasts, advertised as the Hounds of Hell come back to life, were just round yonder bend. But, I remembered my ancestors and knew that the only way to deal with these types is to stand fast and look them straight in the eyes. Algy's monocle quivered as he recalled the moment. "I nearly besmirched myself. I was glad I was wearing my kilt in the true Highland fashion." At that tense juncture there lollopped round the corner two amiable totally shagged out sheepdogs. At the shepherd's frenzied Gaelic cry of "Seize him Rover!" the two toddled over tails a wagging to slobber over Algy's Sghian-Dhu, finally flopping out on his bedubbined boots. So taken was I that I wiped my brow and gasped with relief when it ended.

On a more traditional note he remembered a day in Glen Affric, reputedly the finest glen in Scotland. When the shepherd hailed him and his partner getting out of their car, they went over thinking they were about to get a wigging for illegal parking. However, the man asked them, if they going over Mam Sodhail, and if so would they mind looking out for sheep in the far glen, Gleann nam Fiadh. Before going very far on their outing, they realized it would be impossible to carry out the shepherd's brief. It was one of those horribly dreich days of mist and rain when you are lucky to see the rucksack straps of the man in front of you; so much for the glories of gorgeous Glen Affric.

Nevertheless, they squelched up and down those sodden slopes at the top of which it is reputed a stunning vista opens up of the entire breadth of Scotland from Atlantic to the German ocean. They had to be content with a drenched cairn surrounded by a patch of sodden heather, in which festive surroundings they munched their damp cheese pieces. Totally drookit, they reported back on their unsuccessful mission. Neither sheep nor any other living creature had they seen. The man stood for a moment in the pouring rain before asking, "Ye'll be takin a dram?" It was a question. The astonishing thing Algy said was that, "We actually took about ten seconds to pretend to think about it." Inside the shepherd's house they had whisky, washed down by hot sweet tea. A very satisfying lubricant, said the shepherd; you get the effect of the whisky twice over. To soak up the liquid, they had gargantuan helpings of Dundee cake. It had been a good day after all.

In order to cheer me up Algy told a story against himself which does not appear in any of his books, anthologies or collected works. He was on his way to Killin with a little group of his followers who looked up to him as an authority and historian of the hills. Buoyed up by their praise Algy decided to stop at Callandar for some refreshment and an opportunity to show off. In those days Callandar was famous for being the backdrop for *Dr. Findlay's Casebook* and the cafe where they stopped was called the *Tannochbrae Tea Shoppe*, presumably in the hope of getting some spin-off from the T.V. crazed hordes for it was under this *nom de guerre* that the village was masquerading for the telly,

"Of course," he said among the clutter of the tea cups and dainty pink and lemon cakes, "Callandar is really more important as the last known camp of the Ninth *Hispana* the famous lost legion who marched off into the mists of the glens and disappeared from history." He paused, "The mystery is on a par with that of the Marie Celeste." Very clearly Algy had whetted their appetites and nothing would do but their leader must guide them round the antiquities. They drove back to the East end of the town and inspected a very imposing grassy mound close by the river. It was going to be an improving day.

"This is a typical second century legionary marching camp. Note the square shaped protective wall and *vallum*, that is ditch, which were standard throughout the Empire, and you can see exact replicas of these from Morocco to the Danube. Now see. If you look closely you can spot the main street, the *Via Praetoria*." He pointed to a vague herbaceous line. "There. There you can see the other main street the *Via Decumana*." An almost imperceptible straggle of weeds crossed the other at right angles. "Look there you can just make out the granaries. The Roman soldier had to have his daily bread - he was nigh on being a vegetarian." Algy waved his hand over an entirely blank area. He then walked over to the centre of the enclosed area, his gang following. "I am standing over the most sacred spot in the camp the temple of Mithras where the standards, the eagles of the legion were dedicated on the altar before battle and each soldier pledged his life for his emperor." He pointed to a slab set in a piece of banking. "Now I want you to look closely at this."

So commanding was Algy's delivery that a crowd of most unlikely scholars had joined the group. They looked more like navvies than historians, but nonetheless seemed to be enjoying themselves. So great was their thirst for knowledge that they kept supping at beer cans to quench it. These tins were replenished from a central stock, a carry out bag at their feet with the slogan, "Here's Tae You!" inscribed on it. So rapt was their attention to Algy's message that not even their expert pronging of the top of each can was allowed to break their concentration.

"Please study carefully this votive tablet. If I may scrape away this moss you can just about see the letters." Algy took out a knife and sliced away a furry layer. "Can you see the letters *D.D.N.N. nob Aug.*" Algy underlined with his fingers the faint lettering. This particularly pleased the local students. There was a long gap that appeared blank. "The next bit is almost indecipherable." He coughed here. There was nothing wrong with his chest. It was merely an affectation to show how pleased he was with himself. "But if I spell it out you might see it." He spelt out *H E R E S F E C I T.* With a dash of imagination it was just about possible to imagine something like that there written there.

"What does it mean? It is an ancient Roman grave. The *D.D.N.N.* stands for Domini Nostri - Our Lords Nobillissimi Caesar et Augustus - Noble Caesar and Emperor. This is a reference to the pious emperor Marcus Aurelius and his co-emperor, Lucius Verus, who was also invested with the purple. It was custom for all tombstones in the Roman Empire to refer to the current emperor. The last two words '*Heres fecit*' –is best translated as his heir erected this memorial, and so proves for us that it was such an object.

A burst of applause from the locals was received by Algy with due courtesy. He doffed his cap and blushed briefly at this compliment to his modest display of scholarship. The oldest of the group, who had the air of a wiseacre, asked Algy if he had pen and paper, "Because I must write yon Hocus Pocus doon. I ken the local paper will be really interested in this. What did you say? The last known stopping place in the enigma - How does that spell? - of the ninth legion." He had the sly grin of the village character and began stroking an imaginary beard, as if investing himself with the wisdom of the ages. There was a thin patch of grey stubble on his chin, like hoar frost on an apple. The morning's shave had been fairly rudimentary.

"It's funny really because the boys, and me," he pointed to his beery fellows. Algy sensed trouble in the offing. "We dug this up all aboot fifteen year ago. It was the beginning o' a housin' scheme." He turned to them, "Mind lads." They nodded like Punch. The friends of Algy stood in mute horror, as the sacrilege was unfolded in front of them. "But the surveyor had'nae done his work properly. The river kept floodin'. So we had tae pack it in. The council were up in arms aboot a' the mess, so we hud tae cover up all the rubbish an haulf built walls. We landscaped it. It was a pretty good job. Its fuled a lot o' folk."

"But the inscription?" stammered Algy. "Ins....what? Oh yon. We were haeing a bit a' a laugh wi the village bike Donna Donaldson. Nae Neekers we called her." He pointed to the D.D.N.N. She's now in Glesgae, happy hooring the day away." "I'm pleased to hear it," muttered Algy. He had lost too much ground to point out the misspelling. The old lad's grubby finger tricked along the legend, "Nobbed again. Yon *heres fecit* if you look carefully its 'here.'" He stopped there. A trace of the old

Highland gentility inhibited him from enunciating that last unsavoury word.

The local bullies roared with laughter, while Algy's group stood silent, sharing the shame of this defeat for scholarship. A lesser man than Algy would have crawled away in mortification. There was a short pause. Algy coughed again.

"Friends," he nodded at his opponents, "scholars, what we have here is the perennial fascination of history. The search for and rooting out of clues even in the most insignificant mud heap" – a nice one in the eye - "The diversity of interpretations make history the Queen of Knowledge. The fearless seeker after truth must be prepared to endure the scorn of the illiterate" - steady Algy - "before he finds that chameleon the protean enigma that is history that cloaks the source of Scotland's Antick Glory!"

Ninety per cent of this was absolute Hebrew to the boisterous yokels, but they recognized, even if dimly, a man after their own hearts and gave him a rousing send off. It was one of Algy's best yarns and it was a pity that it was never favoured with publication. Later, one of Algy's chums told me that when they got to Killin that day, their leader lashed them up Ben Lawyers with unusual urgency.

Algy's Love Epic

By Moira Fiorelli

Another night, another song. This time the gramophone was echoing to sounds more authentically Algy, the lament by the great piping family, the MacCrimmons, "Lochaber No More." We were assured from the record sleeve that it was recorded on a sequestered rock on the furthest bounds of Moidart, and was played at sunset - a perhaps unnecessary refinement. Certainly the poignant melody evoked a different response from Algy's picaresque tales. As usual there were plates almost hidden under a pile of variegated cakes. But Algy was in a different mood tonight, almost fidgety. Scones and buns that disappeared from his plate were instantly replaced. He kept running to and fro from the pantry to keep the supply lines open. I had to say, "Whoa! Algy. I won't be able to eat my tea soon. What's the emergency? The bakeries will be open again tomorrow." He turned to me in a state of excitement.

"I am smitten, Moira, I have been smitten and am utterly, utterly reduced." This was so unlike Algy's true nature that he had to express himself in this pantomime language. "Relax, tell me about it." I calmed him down. He sat down and thereupon after much sighing and soughing told me his tale of woe.

He was in a woeful state. The love light was affecting his work. When he sat down to write of his epic trudges across the Cairngorms, his pen feverishly took flight. At the end of two hours it was time for a tea break. He placed his pen in the sugar free tea and slowly stirred through force of habit from his two lump days. As he sipped and supped he felt a lazy tingle of anticipation. He was about to relive his adventures by scanning his prose ahent those vasty plains. There would be half blurred tracks in the snow, blizzard crusted eyebrows, the fierce glint of ice and the blue horizon, eternally tantalizing in its brief advent. He sighed as he lifted the paper. The moment of bliss was upon him.

What was this? He read:

"Roses thine cheeks

Almond thine eyes

The wood at Lynwilg shall surely be thy thighs."

Was he deranged? Had he been haunted by some love-lost damsel jilted by one of his clansmen ancestors? What he did not know at the time and only discovered after several worrying trips to the doctors was that he was suffering from that rarest form of writer's block; the condition know as manic logorrhea or in correct medical terminology the Obsessive Byronic syndrome.

As soon as his pen touched paper, even for a shopping list, there would appear cupids, puttis and treacly little cherubs blowing kisses. A day in the hills written up in his diary appeared as a love-lorn sonnet, in a style know as High McGonigailian. A letter to the Bank Manager was returned stamped. "Sent to wrong address".

He opened,'My Darling Rosebud,

With reference to your previous communication, re your verdant flowery banks and the moistened lips of my overdraft.' He laughed when he showed me this. He was not ashamed. The tyranny and advantage seeking of petty bureaucrats held no terrors for him.

But it was affecting his job or as he characteristically put it, "The place, where I eke out the daylight hours, to gain the miserable pittance that gives me bread for my mouth and food for the hill." "Yes, that's it," I said laughing despite an obviously troubled tale. "Has your logorrhea affected your eking?" It had. He was an architect on a fairly high screw despite his romanticising about "miserable pittances," whose drawings had always been marked by a spare almost Spartan style exceptionally well suited to local Government building. Now, since his affliction, there would appear at each corner of his drawing paper a flower, differing according to mood and season. Pillars came to life as limbs. Sloping roofs erupted into flower adorned, waving tresses with corniches and curlicues; gable ends once bare now sprouted ravishing cinquefoils. Arches, formerly dull semi-circles, were now rampant cuspeds, Floretines or even double arabesques of exquisite loveliness. Swimming baths were alternately hearts or almond eyes. Even a few test stretches of motorway rioted in luscious curves, that were aesthetically pleasing when viewed from a helicopter but tended to make car drivers dizzy and their passengers travel sick. Right-angled triangles were broken so their hypotenuses were turned menacingly inwards towards the dark recesses of the inner right angle.

The partners worried. Algy had long been a loyal uncomplaining employee good at drawing up plans for the cheapest type of building that could stand the pressure of a mild breeze. Now with his artistic fantasies, building costs were rocketing. They decided in that curiously ugly phrase to tough it out. Their rewards were not long in coming. An obscure trade journal printed in Bucharest claimed to see some merit in what it termed the neurosis of phallic architecture. Weeks later learned periodicals from Milan to Chicago were falling over themselves in lavishing praise on the new Corbusier of the Inner Thighs.

The obscure office in Edinburgh where Algy spent his daylight hours was flooded with orders for office blocks, conference centres and agnostic chapels for the Church of England's Left Wing. Walking into the office was a nightmare. Algy was forced to go in a side door disguised as a janitor to avoid the cordon of excitable journalists.

Then quite suddenly it all stopped. Algy was cured. He was out of love and back with us on the hills. He told me, "I came to my senses. Women become old and grey." I raised my eyebrows at this, but I don't think he noticed, so fixed was he in his self-belief. "They are just ephemeral things. The hills, well, they are eternal they never change."

"Except in winter; or haven't you noticed," I said this to myself for there was no use putting him off now that he was back in the fold. He went back to creating the squalid flat-roofed prison huts that modern architecture has seen fit to serve on the modern office worker. The Rund-Bogenstil arches reminiscent of the thighs of the Valkurie maidens disappeared replaced by concrete slab lintels specifically ordered by the Corporation to depress their tenants. The partners were delighted. It had all been a bit too giddy; besides he was once more cost conscious. Martina Drawley in the Guardian tried to proclaim him the Spartacus of the Building Site, but it was no good. The show was over. The merry moment had passed.

Who was this woman who had caused so much turbulence? How was he later cured from his bewitching by the "Goddess in the Green Silk Dress" as he called her? Algy told me she lived near the Calton Hill. I made a joke "Not in the Tolbooth" - that was the old city jail. "No, no not all," he was deadly serious, and I could see this was no time for frivolity.

"What does she do then?" I said to mollify him.

"She's a swimming bath attendant."

"A what?" It was news to me that Algy was amphibious. "When do you go swimming?" Algy confessed that in his few leisure moments, by which he meant when he was not climbing or writing, his job being just an irritating detail that filled the weekdays, he liked to go to Portobello Baths, situated in middle class Joppa, which were renowned for the health giving property of their briny waters, and where he found that lying soaking in the warm baths he could muse creatively about the hills, their history and legends.

It was a Monday afternoon when he first saw her. The weekend scrambling over the many limbs of the Mamore ridges had been tiring but rewarding. He wanted to wash away the aches while mulling over the miles hiked, wild life spotted and personalities met. In the empty pool the water was hardly lapping. Standing stock still on the edge of the springboard was a Cretan goddess as sculpted by Phidias with russet hair pouring down her back like a flame. The light dappled and lilting fluttered like a mosaic across her face. She raised her arms, eyes fixed on the empty air above the water. She sprang, jack-knifed, sliced and churned the water. Circular rings spread, bounced back and collided. In that instant the damage was done for Algy.

Up till now Algy had only seen the female form heavily disguised under winter climbing clothes, balaclavas, baggy anoraks and unflattering climbing breeches. This new experience had been shattering. In fact Algy fell into the pool and nearly drowned. The Water Goddess had to dive back in and pilot him to the shore. Fortunately for Algy's nervous system she had not yet learnt the kiss of life, but brought him back to consciousness by the vigorous, but back wrenching Holger-Neillson method. I heard the story from the lady herself and I have no reason to disbelieve it. She told me all this in a quite matter of fact voice, as if rescuing poets was all in a day's work.

It was in many ways an ideal form of introduction. Algy quickly exploited this close encounter to chat up the lady. Like all others who met him, she instantly took a liking to the gentleman scholar. She had never before come across anyone remotely like him for debonair charm, eccentricity and general zest for life. On his subsequent and now more frequent visits to the baths she found herself irresistibly taken by his purposeful flat dive into the water and the deterrent effect it had on the other bathers. His porpoise like motion towards the other end of the bath only helped to confirm her affections.

The love affair in the baths, however, was not destined to flourish. Their feelings for each other ran on parallel but quite distinct lines. As an aesthete and an intellectual, Algy treasured her as a beautiful object such as a Ming vase or a Pre-Raphaelite painting to be looked at and adored. Indeed he described her as if she was one of Dante Gabriel Rossetti's ladyloves. When I at last met this *object d' arte*, I saw that she fell far short of this ideal despite her name, Belle-Anne with its hint of piquant Victoriana. We took an instant dislike to each other by the way. Her interests and personality were purely pragmatic, and prosaic. There was no poetic soar of flight and fancy in her. As far as I was concerned, it hardly merited a bus trip across the city to unravel the wonders of her charm, never mind constant immersion in lukewarm waters.

She chewed gum relentlessly while she drank her lager and blackcurrant cocktail. Her conversation was limited to, "That dress you're wearing is braw. Where did you buy it?" But her eyes told a different story and I soon got fed up with clothes talk. After all she had not got the class to shop at Jenners and I had no idea where the dingy shops were that she frequented. They could have been in Leith Docks for all I knew.

Her greeting to him that night was, "And hoo's the heather on the hill then, Alg?" His eyes sparkled; I shuddered. Her fascination for Algy was limited to his novelty value and physical prowess in the baths. Mind you she was impressed with the opulence of his towel, which showed that she was not entirely short of her marbles. It was hard work for Algy as his dates were almost entirely confined to the baths, which had a noticeable affect on the texture of his skin. His face was becoming chapped and it looked as if he was wearing prune skin gloves. Once quite unabashed she announced, "Your poem's like oor gairden in need of a good weeding." This was in reference to "There were Tulips on Traprain," which appears in all the major anthologies and inspired the Scotsman poetry critic to dub him "The Rabid Burns of our Mountains." I was horrified to hear this blasphemy. Algy merely gave an enraptured chuckle.

His solitary date outside the baths was a significant landmark in the story of his romance. They were going to a Gala evening at the Carousel. For the occasion the in-house band had been practicing Strauss waltzes. To the old fashioned swaying rhythms they had added the thrum of guitars and pulsing bongo drums to allow for the selective taste of their clientele.

Algy turned up to meet her in full dress Highland regalia, a frilled cravat at the collar of his black dress jacket. As a token of his troth he was wearing in his buttonhole a sprig of purple scented heather. Belle-Anne was wearing a green silk gown with a high Chinese collar, which emphasized her swan like neck. The gown, which was full and flowing, swished and rustled as she walked, making aphrodisiac music. Algy was spellbound. Being a Gala night she had left her chewing gum at home. As he had not said anything for two minutes, usually a sign that he was asleep she poked him and said, "Come on Algy, let's swim for it." For years after you had only to mention the word swim for Algy's eyes to prick with tears.

The evening was not entirely a success. Algy could wobble with the best of them, but he could not gogo at all. To him the repertoire of the modern dance hall was limited and tedious in the extreme. The patrons of the Carousel on the other hand were not used to Highland War Whoops or energetic sword dances. The regular suave bouncer was on holiday in Torremolinos. He had the urbane ability of removing troublesome customers without causing too much of a stir. "Come, come, sir, I think a spot of fresh air wouldn't do us any harm. Don't you?" Before the culprit could say, "Jack Robinson" or "Hey Jimmy" a hand would be placed round the scruff of his collar another round the seat of his pants and he would be whisked expeditiously out of the hall into the fresh Morningside night air.

Some local cowboys with fantasies of belonging to a junior section of the Mafia, were doing the job as a sort of *locum tenens*. With their broad-brimmed Fedora hats, hands thrust menacingly in their jacket pockets and coughing up bits of splintered cigars, they only looked ridiculous. They were making a mistake in taking on Algy. Normally the most peaceable of men, but with his blood raised up, in his tartan gear and dancing the Gay Gordons he could have stood in the line with Wolfe on the Heights of Abraham. Their tactless, "Listen, Hamish, no-one wants to see your knickers" caused the incident. I must say I have some sympathy with Belle-Anne in making herself scarce during this embarrassing scene. After all some of her clients at the baths might have witnessed it.

There was only a short scuffle. The aspirant cammoristi and Algy soon agreed that there was a misunderstanding on both sides. When Algy got round to telling them that the Young Pretender was a domiciled Italian one sensed that the trouble was over. After shaking hands with them all, Algy set forth on his hunt for Belle-Anne. He soon found her dancing in the arms of a brickie. Those almond eyes, catalyst of so much poetry and outdoor swimming pools were sparkling, as he had never seen them. They were afire with lust. That dress shimmered and floated as she turned to reveal legs the like of which he had only seen attached to bathing costumes. When for a moment she cast a glance at Algy's sad face, the look she gave was disdainful. As he said, "I might as well have been on the top of An Teallach." This sharp reminder of the scene of my own desolation gave me a painfully vivid insight into how he felt. "I know how you feel," I said. He looked straight into my eyes. For a moment I saw a man, not the comic cuts caricature I create to keep the world at bay.

Attempts to phone her later were met by rebuffs. Her mother answered the phone and refused to admit that Algy had any claim on her daughter's time. "Belle-Anne is otherwise engaged," was her laconic, uninformative, unvarying reply. Neither wonder Algy was in a state. Unlike me he had a constructive method of getting over it, by using his malady as a weapon. February 14th was approaching.

To a man like him infected with rampant Byronism it was only a matter of minutes to dash off an ode entitled "The Ballad of Belle-Anne," with the subtitle of "Yon Lassie in the Green Silk Dress," and pop it in with a Valentine card. The ode made some flattering comparisons of the Swimming Bath Attendant with divae of the Silvery screen. Most of them were people I had never heard of, Theda Barra, Hedy Lamar and Jean Harlow, which made me wonder about Algy's age. The only response to this was a graceless request to borrow his dictionary. Algy was not in the least deterred. He was like Robert the Bruce's spider. Night after night he went back to the Carousel to that space where he had last sat with his adored Belle-Anne. He never moved. It was enough to recreate that evening, at least the early part of it. Girls even took to asking him to dance, for he was not without a certain raffish appeal. But he always demurred politely and with gentility as befits the scion of an old Scottish House. This was mildly sad, because it only left a few girls hearts softly fluttering, thinking what might have been, and frankly they sounded a lot more suitable than Belle-Anne Mac Grub.

His lonely sentinel picket became such a feature of the Carousel that the management, now regretting their earlier impulse to expel the Highlander, brought him refreshments. He became once again a minor celebrity. The attendance improved, especially among the better class of young ladies with a soulful disposition. On the billboard outside under the name of the group "The Birlin' Boulders," they pasted on in quite large lettering, "Spend Saturday night with the Greyfriars Bobby of Morningside."

But for Algy a more serious campaign was under way. After the route of his ode, he was planning to assault her with a full-length novel, no less. Unlike the poem, it was a work that she might read. He set himself the task of composing a Bodice Ripper. With his usual thoroughness he addressed himself to the requisite research sitting up in bed after his nightly communion at the Carousel, reading volume upon volume of torrid passion consummated quiveringly under an exotic night sky or rather not quite, for virginity was at a premium in these fantasies. The fateful thrust was delayed at least till the last chapter and only after the purchase of a gold ring, but most often took place only in the reader's thoughts after she had closed the book's covers with an enraptured sigh. In case you want to follow his development more closely, I give you here a selection from his reading list. "Lily at Midnight," "With a Brigand on the Bare Mountain," "Even Passion Flowers Wilt," "The Nun of Mount Athos," "I Lost my Gucci Handbag" and the book he used as a model, "A Torment of Thighs", for which it was claimed, falsely I think, to have been recently translated from the Persian. All these are I am assured, easily available at the better airport bookshops.

The book was to be called, "The Green Silk Dress" - what else? In it Belle-Anne the heroine was thinly disguised as Anna of the Dales. The setting was the massage parlour of the Turkish Baths in the spa town of Buxton. Knowing the character of the lady and her occupation it was pretty obvious that she was being taken off. I warned Algy it might be actionable, but this only served to encourage him. The possibilities of the location were exploited with a sly humour that came as a surprise to me. For instance, if a customer requested a blow job, Anna-A-Dale would say "Certainly sir, in just a minute," and leave the hopeful lying tingling under his towel with excitement. When she returned with her breasts pouting under her blouse, the client was frothing with anticipation. Smiling sweetly she lifted up the towel and pressed a red-hot hair dryer against his nether regions. It was all done very skillfully, the sexual functions only being alluded to following the strict conventions of the genre.

On her nights off Anna went to the Buxton Plaza. Swirling around in her green silk dress she soon took over the middle of the floor. A gang of jack-booted bikers surrounded her bouncing off their knees in an unfit imitation of Cossack Dancers, while she clicked her fingers, stomped her feet and thrashed her hair around, the only Flamenco dancer in the Peak District. Because she came from Yorkshire, she always carried a white rose between her teeth.

The bodice ripper like all the true art forms had its own strict formula and even a precise lexicon. Bodily functions were restricted to eating, drinking and hot-blooded looks. Algy told me he found it very exhausting sticking to the rules. Religiously restricting himself to the allotted phrases it took all his strength of character to see it through to the end. "It's a discipline no doubt about that, Moira." When I read the manuscript with its "bosoms brimming with passion," and "his ardent thrusting crushed her petal like lips" I thought it had been written by a lovesick computer, whose programmed vocabulary had been put on an economy diet.

91

The most fascinating discovery Algy unearthed was the elegance and simplicity of the genre's structure, which was unvarying and pure as a mathematical theorem. It was based on the eternal triangle of two women and one man. The man, usually a Texas millionaire with a love of Degas and Gucci leatherwork, was a workaholic forever dashing hither and thither on errands of commerce round the globe. So tight was his schedule that whenever he alighted be it Abu-Dhabi or Prestwick all his meetings had to be conducted in the airport's VIP lounge, where his own brand of champagne was always kept on ice in case he dropped out of the skies unexpectedly. His shirts, specially monogrammed by a discretely tailoring establishment in Saville Row, were worn straight from the cellophane packet and its attendant pins. Used shirts, one must suppose, were flushed down the aircraft's loos.

The alternative hero was a shy Scottish laird who never went further than the lowliest shieling on his estate. His world was a large draughty castle, surrounded by the grim memorabilia of his warlike ancestors. He had only recently learned to speak English, preferring to be closeted with his fiercely nationalistic head factor parleying in Gaelic. That he was not an imbecile, in this habitat was somewhat surprising. Yet his brooding taciturnity in alliance with his darkly handsome looks had wrung the hearts of secretaries and governesses from Chelsea to Oldham.

Fighting for the attention of either of these lads were the two girls. The odds-on favourite was a stunningly beautiful blonde with legs like a racehorse. She too favoured Gucci shoes and scarves. Her underwear was invariably hand-painted Japanese silk, and the mere glimpse of her satiny bra strap in the early scenes was enough to depress the heroine and make her consider entering a nunnery. This other girl a gamine, red head or brunette, lacked her rival's elegant clothes sense and always considered her looks ill favoured until a perceptive raising of eye by Texan or Gael caused a consequent reddening of a hitherto unadmired cheek. The heroine could usually be recognised by her oily hands through working on her motorbike or tractor. In the unusual event of her having lily white hands there was always the crisp white blouse that she wore, so displaying at once her virginity and practical common sense. She always won through in the end, somewhat unfairly I thought, because the ravishing beauty was either the hero's sister, dying of consumption or had blotted her copy book by showing too eager an interest in consummation without benefit of clergy, suspicions might also have been aroused by the false heroines being too conversant with the exchange rate between Dollars American and Pounds Scots.

Algy decided to turn the conventions on their head by inverting the triangle. Two men, a Texas millionaire and a not so shy Scottish laird were the unlikely customers at the Turkish Baths. Both were suitors for the hands of the massage maid; these very hands which regularly thumped their vertebrae and soothed their skin afterwards with expensive unguents. Once in a while they fought duels as to who was to be first on the rubbing table, which took place in the misty moors above the gritstone edges. Descriptions of pistols at dawn over Stanage Edge enabled **Algy** to splash out on a few scenes of Wuthering Heights intensity.

Anna, taking the rose out of her teeth would laugh with scorn at the two desperate men. When not on duty in the dance hall or **massage** parlour she wore a crisp white blouse. Hidden under this blouse but hinted at by a whiff of expensive perfume was a ravishing set of Giannina Ridotto undies. Thus she fulfilled the qualifications and personalities of both the girls in the standard texts in her single self. Occasionally rubbing oil from the massage parlour remained stuck under her fingernails. This had to do for motorbike grease.

It was not published. Algy had flouted the conventions. The publishers sensed that his heart was not in it and suspected that the literary pseudonym that he had taken, Georgina von Anker was a micky take. The fact that the readers were expected to take a vote on who would win the heart of the lady seemed to indicate a loss of interest on the part of the author. Algy protested that calling on a readers' survey was a very topical way of involving his public in literary creativity. The chairman of the firm shook his head sorrowfully. Algy's prose had given his wife and him several evenings of mirth, but his commercial instinct knew it would be a disaster.

I think it was just as well. Belle-Anne might well have read it in her spare moments by the poolside. Her brother, whose friends were rather a rough lot, had taken an over-possessive dislike to Algy's bathing habits. Anyway its purpose was served, for the act of creation had burnt away his passion.

Much later, when he had earned a modest niche in the Hall of Fame, his admirers spoke of a lost book, an unearthed masterpiece that revealed the soul of the master, and there was even talk of a search for the secret folios. Luckily for his reputation a more than usually alert charlady spotted what she called a load of rubbish in the back of the cupboard she was clearing. She burnt the lot in the compost heap at the bottom of the walled garden. History records that he took it rather well, muttering to himself, "Echoes of Carlyle's servant." A remark his charlady failed to understand. "Some o' Mr. MacBeth's friends are awfy rich wi' servants an a'," she said. "Is that a fact?" replied the friendly gossip over the fence. Her pals activities with a duster in the well appointed houses in Bruntsfield often brought to light many interesting items for their morning blether.

Algy Takes on the Andes

By Moira Fiorelli

Reading the obituary of a close friend is an unsettling experience. Every fact, anecdote, or story, seen through someone else's eyes is out of focus, like the undertaker's rearrangement of the face of a loved one. Thumbing through Algy's obituaries, I noted a thread of misconceptions. For example, calling him a ladies' man was a bit of a stretch, especially when compared with some of the serious knobhounds he was up against in his day. Mind you after being in the hills overlong, he would occasionally emerge Swan like, strutting up and down Prince's Street, seriously suited with a carnation in his lapel, for all the world a Burlington Bertie *sans* spats, to venture voraciously after the fair sex. These *affaires* were not of long standing, and I think a fairer description of him would be a born bachelor, if that were not such a dangerous euphemism nowadays, enjoying outbursts of libido during his rutting season. Sadly these episodes invariably ended in calamity, but Algy remained unbowed. "Bruce and the spider. Bruce and the spider, Moira." Before saying, "Amen to all that," and heading towards his much loved Mamores.

The following episode I think perfectly distills his experience in the *cherchez la femme* quarter. It is little known even within Algy's circle, which is in itself unusual, as he was never falsely modest about his exploits, a hypocrisy he couldn't abide, and included him pulling off a remarkable first ascent in an otherwise unremarkable climbing career that for one short glorious moment put him up there with Rheinhold Messner, Walter Bonatti and Hermann Buhl, but in order to spare the reputation of the lady involved he asked me not to publish it till after his demise. I thought it would be more appropriate to wait till the lady was no more, and so I will just call her Cynthia.

The style of the manuscript is an unusual mix. The first part is almost lyrical, with faint traces of his Byronic Period; the actual events on the mountain, the part readers will be interested in, are retailed in a terse staccato format, as if he were ordering a Double Big Mac Meal with extra fries and onion rings on the side from his Hummer in a busy drive through restaurant.

But without further ado:

"It was cold that year in the Tetons. So cold they called it the year with the hole in the middle, the months from June to September only appearing on the calendar for form's sake. August was ushered in with a snow storm and two nights later, unable to sleep on iron hard ground, I got up at four in the morning wrapped my sleeping bag round my shoulders like these old Indian Braves being marched onto the reservation, and for want of anything better to do, trudged down to the water-front.

Merde! Sitting stock still in a frozen yoga pose, was Cynthia contemplating her mantra; a bummer if I ever knew one, as her egocentric vibes would refuse to let her see my being in the vicinity as anything less than crowding her space. By this time her antennae would have picked up my presence, even though she never moved her eyes off of the hills beyond the water, as if protocol demanded her not recognizing my existence. But I kept on moving. Who knows what she would have thought if I had scuttled away. I looked at her sitting outside the tent trying to keep warm on that failure of a summer's night, and was instantly smitten, her hair, the grey telltale eyes, the texture and smell of her skin, the gentle undulations of her body all contributing to my downfall. She turned round to face me, and as if a cloud had dropped upon the sun, hatred suffused that adorable visage. This instantaneous dislike happens quite often and is something I have learned to live with. Funnily enough I can't say that I liked her either, but then it is a fact oft commented upon by losers that love and hate can coexist in cozy proximity. I sat down just in time to see the sun touching the mist that was like a warm cotton eiderdown blanketing the surface of the water. It must have been the merest scintilla of heat that was all that was required, for quite suddenly wraiths of mist rose up as if orchestrated and we were at the New Year's Ball in Vienna with ladies in brilliant white dresses silently waltzing across the silvery surface of the Grande Opera ballroom. This effect lasted a good twenty minutes and then vanished entirely leaving the surface of the water an uncluttered chilly blue, but during this spectral dance we forgot our enmity, and basked in the ephemeral bond created by the shared aesthetic experience.

'Wasn't that incredible?' I said to keep the moment going.

'Yep.'

In the interests of fairness I have to mention our shared moment. It wasn't much and from that moment our good mateship slid inexorably downhill. Forced to climb together by our mutual friends, we tried to forestall the inevitable clash of two hopelessly incompatible personalities tied together on the same rope. Climbing is nerve racking enough without the added stress of having to overcome a silent cargo of criticism sizzling through the rope, and I for one could never overcome the attacks transmitted through that cord's fiber optic. I managed to climb Baxter's pinnacle unscathed, more-or-less. On the last pitch my hand began making darting movements towards the peg, when I heard an accusatory cough from the stance and the offending limb scampered back onto more legitimate but less palpable holds, and I ascended in a series of nervy frog hops. Really I didn't mind, as pegs are to my hands like a bottle to a drinker's and so renunciation was good for my character. To cap it all that day the view from the top was superb, but I entranced by Cynthia's glorious figure, not understated with her wasp-waist harness, was torn Siren like away, only wishing to put my hands where my eyes were resting.

For a couple more routes my nerves were jangling as much as the pro swinging from my belt. It was not masculine assertiveness, which granted me the hard bits only the spin and fall of a coin. When I fluffed, which I did more and more because of the acute stage nerves from which I was now suffering, I had the dubious pleasure of watching her float upwards like a puffball in a light breeze. Then we did the big one, Irene's Arête on Disappointment Peak. Perhaps the day was just too good for any petty criticism to survive or maybe by the law of averages we had struck a good mood, for even on the hard pitches, where my skill level just barely topped the Plimsoll Line of difficulty, there was no censure; no little daggers of hatred probing the back of my skull. She even threw in one or two words of praise, thinking a scolding would make me miss my footing. For one glorious pitch, stepping out on a skyscraper of rock, it was allowed that I climbed well. I was singing out to the heavens, in tune with the wonderful world, in love with this rock, in love with Cynthia and wondering whether it was possible that she liked me just a little today.

We were late at the summit. To the west the sky was drenched in buckets of blood a sure sign for the dilatory. In the dark, the way down was complex, nasty and dangerous. For the first time we looked into each other's eyes without rancor and saw only the echo of each other's fears. Quickly sorting out the rappel stations I took charge. Cynthia was in a nervous swoon and strangely compliant. Rappelling in the dark on an unknown mountain is not my cup of tea, but can be done as long as you don't try to hurry, and keep your wits about you. Somehow I managed to get both of us down. We hit the path without warning and suddenly were safe. Cynthia collapsed against me crying and threw her arms against my neck. I could feel her body trembling against mine in spasms of shock and relief. The moonlight threw our shadows together across the path. I took this as an invitation.

By George, was I ever wrong! She stopped and pushed me away, 'You bastard!' She made a quick recovery did Cynthia, and then went on with a well-stocked lexicon of aspersions. If she had shrieked 'rapist!' into the woods I couldn't have felt worse. I coiled up the rope and trudged down the path, glad that the darkness was swallowing up my cheeks that were burning so brightly I hardly needed a flashlight. I was whistling madly as per instructions to keep the bears at bay, but in reality doing some urgent repair work on my shattered moral-fiber.

The next day we said goodbye at the airport Hertz rental counter, exchanging the usual remote cheek brushing brand of kiss, a hollow parody of the one I had tried to seize the day before. Even in that impersonal terminal I felt the mild electric shock akin to fear that triggers arousal, but her eyes were looking at the clock and that cold alabaster skin was as alive as Nefertiti. Neither of us could bring ourselves to say, 'Nice to have met you.' Her eyes were saying. 'Like Hell it was!' As she drifted off down the corridor I thought, 'Well, that's the last of Cynthia,' shrugged my shoulders and turned away."

Which made it all the more surprising when two years later, Algy received the following note from Cynthia. Odder still it was addressed to;

The Hon. Algernon McBrayne Macbeth of that Ilk,

Thane of Cawdor,

Glamis Castle,

Somewhere near Brigadoon,

Scotland,

And reached him at his bijou residence in Morningside Edinburgh.

"Hi Algy!

"Remember me! And what a sweet ole time we had in the Tetons and that romantic stroll in the moonlight after Irene's Arête. You were climbing brilliantly that day, but what else is new." Not quite his recollection, but he decided to read on. "It were me nose, led me, Moira. If I had an ounce of common, I'd have thrown letter on the fire."

"But you're smokeless?"

"Well, I can hardly say I threw it on the radiator."

"Do you fancy expeditioning with me, my husband and several close friends, all mountaineers of élan to climb the Last Great Problem of the Andes, The Pillar of Fire on Huascaran? Of course you do, and apart from the joy of your company, your rock skills are needed for the crux. My husband, who you have so much in common with, can't wait to meet his predecessor. Reply quickly.

The pear is ripe.

Your Cynthia."

It says much for Algy's optimism regarding human nature that he took her word at face value, packed his rucksack, left a note for his daily, and took the first flight to Lima.

....

Algy looked up at the prospective route, a glittering cutlass of ice suspended over horrendous precipices. Of the advertised rock there was merely a couple of brown blotches. His look at Cynthia was returned with a shrug of the shoulders. "Well, steep ice is a Scotchman's second home, huh?"

"Jacta est alea: the die is cast."

"Eh?"

"Caesar said that crossing the Rubicon."

"Sure he did, Algy. Sure he did."

That evening Algy was presented with a huge vat of wheaty German beer. "That's for being such a good sport about the rock's non-appearance, Alg." He had already been a sport about her putting her spouse's name on his own mountain permit, for her husband had to put off his prospective delight at meeting Algy, having fallen prey to a nasty bug that had sent him home, and there wasn't time to be bothered bribing the authorities about a Scotsman being smuggled onto an entirely American expedition. The beer was cloudy and wheaty, anathema to Algy, who was allergic to wheat products, but he didn't say anything so as not to offend Cynthia, and, who besides being the only other white climber on the trip, appeared to be the leader of the gang.

That night he had a nightmare about rearranging the deck chairs aboard the Titanic. He woke up gasping and clutched at Cynthia, "Hey buddy boy, don't get ideas. We're sharing the tent to cut down on loads and prevent temperature dissipation. No other facilities permitted!" Algy, who had never before been at such a high altitude, was suffering from Cheyne-Stokes breathing, a horrible experience when the climber wakes up thinking he is drowning, apologized like the gentleman he was. "Of course, terribly, terribly sorry," Algy wheezed still very discomposed, "A thousand apologies and all that.

"Just keep them roving hands in your own warm space." Algy was mortified, but there was little a drowning sailor desperately trying to surface could do.

Next day he felt wretched, as if a bad case of flu was sitting on top of the mother of all hangovers. This part of the expedition was a trudge up a tedious moraine, relieved by huge smooth boilerplate slabs, which as they were steeply tilted required a certain amount of balance work. Algy was tottering so much the porters insisted on taking his pack off him in case he slipped. Again Algy was mortified, being treated as a sissy, but had to face the brutal fact that he couldn't do it with a load.

Camp 1 was on a bleak grey snowfield, surrounded by all the detritus of a retreating glacier. "George Bush, get a load of this." Algy thought. He could not face dinner, so retreated into his gloomy tent and chilly pit. He couldn't sleep; only dozed between shivering fits. Darkness fell like a curtain call, when there was a rustle of tent flaps, the whir of zippers being unfastened, and there was Cynthia blocking out the last of the light. "Don't get any ideas." She was removing her anorak, and in the press of the tent her breasts smothered Algy's face, causing a different set of breathing problems. Off came sweater and shirt, duvet trousers and long silk combinations. Algy had heard about Victoria's Secret models from his more sexually excitable comrades, and suddenly there was one sitting next to him, complete with minimalist bra and microscopic satin panties, which barely could be seen to be believed. "It took all of my training as a Scottish Public School Gentleman to remain master of myself, Moira. I thought of the grim dank walls of Clachaig Gully in the rain, but even that did not calm the raging of my tadger, as the flowers in the Gully matched the frilly patterns of her bra. I summoned up sad Sunday mornings in the Kirk and so reached quietus.'

But then surprise, surprise.

"Hi Algy, Scots wha hae and all that. Is the old lion still rampant?" This weathervane of a woman had him confuddled and confused, but in the end he was a man not a monk.

'Moira, what could I do. This was a direct challenge to my Scottish manhood. So I said, "If you're English, go spike yourself on my Bannockburn pike."

"Algy, you are something else!" And she grabbed me meat and two veg. Etc, etc...suffice to say that I had to crawl out the tent the next morning.'

There was no load carrying for Algy that day, as it was deemed a rest day, and the party retreated to base camp amongst the donkey shat-upon meadows well below the snow line. Visitors arrived at the campsite, a shifty bunch of climbers intent on a nearby peak. One of them was a doctor, dirty and unshaven a relentless leerer down the front of Cynthia's blouse. Algy resolved to eat an apple a day. Cynthia made a great to do about their welcome, sprucing herself up delightfully, and insisting to his mystification on introducing him as her husband. Algy was thinking if I can do one half of the job, I am entitled to the other half, thus helping him regain said appetite. He dined prodigiously, almost draining the stock of Peruvian wine, needed to aid the passage of the alpaca steaks on their digestive journey. His playmate was playfully tickling his tadger under the table, setting his loins on fire and so counteracting the good work of his digestive juices.

'Kings may be blest, but Algy *was glorious,*

O'er all the ills of life victorious.'

But later, when he staggered to her tent that night after regaling the campsite with his on the spot rendering of Tam O'Shanter, the zipper was firmly snapped shut. Was she a closet Englishwoman? The abrupt change in policy was explained to him lucidly. "Keep your kilt on, big boy. No oatcakes for supper tonight."

The next day Algy roaring like a Berserker deprived of his daily pillage, stormed up the hill to camp 1, and ripped apart the fly sheet on the coy lass' tent, where in another baffling reversal of policy, she warmly welcomed him into her boudoir. Dimly he sensed that this was not feminine fickleness, but a consistent line of attack designed to keep Tom Tiddler furiously ablaze. Another tremendous bout of rogering brought Algy to such ecstatic heights he winged himself to the top of the mountain. His feelings for Cynthia were muddled; on the one hand he saw she was a bad lot, on the other he had been sucked into a vortex of irrevocable passion, and felt he was being dragged into the nether pits of the Inferno by his Eurydice.

But what it did for his ego. He said to himself, "Who now dares call me a boring old bookworm?" And then shouted out to the mountain, "I am a lover: I am a rake, I am a shagger of women." And he resolved there and then that when he returned to ground zero he would burn all his clothes, and attire himself in the outfit of a boulevardier, of a roisterer, cutting swathes through the ranks of Edinburgh Spinsterhood with his well seasoned tadger. With these noble resolutions in mind, he fell into a deep satisfying sleep, quite forgetting he had to get up at two am for the summit assault.

The sun was just warming the fabric of the tent, when he awoke. It was 6 o'clock, desperately late for the summit. His lover's hand was insinuating itself round his bottom. Immediately his truncheon snapped to attention.

"Not now, honeysuckle. Wait till after the summit." But the look on her face told him this was no lovey-dovey moment. Cynthia wore the grim visage of a she-devil wafting baleful waves of hatred. One hand was pinching his bottom, while the other was held high about to pierce him with a hypodermic syringe containing a suspicious, pea green mixture.

"What the devil!" This was no nurse; this was Brutus making the final stab. Quickly realizing his life was in danger, he rolled over to the wall of the tent letting loose a cascade of ice chips produced by condensation onto both of them. That slowed her down momentarily but she was gripping his botty like a mad dog, poised to strike with the poisonous needle.

All his life Algy had been a fanatically tidy person, from the days when he neatly tucked his teddy bear in with his pajamas when a little lad in boarding school. His one lazy moment saved his life. The Nalgene Pee bottle had been left open after use. Algy grabbed it and threw the liquid in the lady's face. She dropped the syringe, clutched her face and howled and screamed with histrionics worthy of the Phantom of the Opera. Algy grabbed the needle, rammed it up her butt, and triggered the plunger. He only managed to get it half in as she writhed and struggled buckling the needle with maniacal strength. Her eyes rolled up. Suddenly her body started jerking and convulsing, as she went into a horrible fit, gasping, coughing and retching for breath. What was in that needle? Her twitching slowed down and settled into deep sleep, although her breathing sounded like a rattling bag of bones, but she was now coughing up large frothy piles of sputum, like a cappuccino machine gone haywire.

As her spasms subsided Algy pondered on what she was up to. It clicked. All that pretending he was her husband for the sake of the pass was a load of cods wallop. Then that wheaty beer, high altitude rogering and finally the needle. Cynthia wanted to kill him off by infecting him with pulmonary edema, claim him to be her husband, and no doubt scarper off with a hefty insurance payout. It was a brilliant plan, the perfect mountaineering murder! Taking no chances, he cut down the long guy ropes, and then tied her to the tent pole. She woke up coughing, and grasping the situation immediately her face went deathly white. Algy held up the needle. "What's it all about then, Cynthia?"

"It wasn't my idea."

"So where is your husband?"

Silence.

Algy brought the needle within stabbing distance to her bottom.

"Ok. At this moment he is probably settling down under the knife before getting facial reconstruction in a clinic in Brazil. The fee would come out of the insurance money that you were going to provide us with."

"And he has changed his name?"

"Yes. We were thinking of giving him your name. But that would mean he would have to act like a complete idiot." She paused nervously, but Algy's eyes never even flickered. "In about three months we will be setting up business serving coffee with cocaine in an Internet cafe in Paraguay."

Hubby had made serious investment errors, and the Mob had sent him several seriously worded reminders. Cynthia remembered that in a poor light Algy sort of looked like him, and knowing him to be a poor booby had invited him along on this mountaineering shagathon. The one monthly premium for the life insurance had set them back so much they had had to sell their trophy house in New Albany. Everything was staked in this one desperate throw. She had got the idea watching Algy sneezing when coming down the forest after the Grand Teton. The needle contained a veritable Pandora's Box of asthma producing allergens that would kill their victim by mimicking pulmonary edema, a common cause of high altitude mortality.

"There's still enough in here to kill?" She nodded nervously.

"If you kill me you will never get off this mountain alive. Even if you don't, you won't. Every porter is like a trained killer, ex-Shining Path, and itching to do you in. To them you are a fat-assed Scottish Landlord, oppressing serfs and screwing their wives." She added conversationally. "They cut their victims' heads off." Algy had wondered why the supposedly jolly porters were always scowling at him. 'This is a rum do.' He thought. 'In thon muddy creek without a paddle.' Even at this extremity, when I saw her all tied up I felt a tinkle in me tadger. Must have a thing about bondage. Funny things you learn about yourself when you're in the pickle jar."

His mind cleared. All the way up he had wondered why this splendid woman was mad for him. Algy had few illusions about his potential as a gigolo. He was the poor booby they had set him up to be. Well, he was stuck with that. That explained the peculiar Mogambo incident at base camp, when she had got all dressed up *a la* Grace Kelly in that floaty blue chiffon affair. That was to impress the seedy pox doctor, who presumably would be commandeered to sign the death certificate that she and Algy were Love's Young Dream, and later when Algy was desperately clawing after his greens, to tantalize him so he would be horny as a goat high on the mountain, bursting heart and lungs to join the Andes High Altitude Leg-over Club.

He looked at Cynthia now not Grace Kelly but still desirable in a Jane of the Jungle sort of way, much better fodder than the roly-poly Indio lasses at the base of the mountain. How about a revenge shag for old times sake, as hardship payment, he wondered, but immediately put it out of mind, imagining the reaction of his female friends. Rape however spelt, was an ugly word. Anyway he needed all his juices for his escape.

"There's three camps to get through, where everyone plus the camp cook is eager to chop off that wandering willy of yours. The death certificate will say pulmonary edema, however your mince is cooked." Cynthia croaked out effortfully. "You're like so totally screwed." She had that smug smirk on her face wine waiters have when they slip you vinegar, when you ordered champagne," was how Algy put it.

"You won't kill me. You haven't the balls for it." For Algy this was truly a sore point. He winced as he told me, recalling the injuries done to his nether parts, all for the sake of lust. "Anyway you're dead, lover boy. Pity in a way, as you weren't such a bad cork stopper. Your body will be tipped into a crevasse, and emerge in like a thousand years time. Maybe sooner if they don't sort out this global warming. Is there any special prayer you want?" She chuckled wheezily.

She had him over a barrel. Could he take her down as a hostage? No. He had no gun and needed both hands to down climb. He was well and truly snookered! Unless? He turned his eyes up to the horrendous buttress swelling above him. Everyone on the mountain was his enemy, and the only way out was to solo to the summit through desperate terra incognita. From close to, he could see rocky patches interrupting the ice. But solo! And him just an average weekender when all is said and done. Even a Bonatti would be hard pressed. But hard battles make for easy choices. "What's your pleasure, Sir? Certain death or almost certain death?" He pocketed a couple of Kendal Mint Cakes, a handful of power bars and two bottles of Gatorade, checked his kit for bivvy sac, pit, headlamp, and fixed his crampons to his boots, not taking much care whether he stamped on her or not. As he told me later, the only way to come to terms with the desperation of the situation was to translate it into a simple routine of doing what came necessary.

"Are you going to kill me?" She wailed suddenly losing all her spunk. He shook his head, waggled the syringe in front of her and stuck it into the floor of the tent. "You're not worth the guilt trip, Sweetie." Then after tying the girl more firmly to the pole he shoved her feet in her sleeping bag and considerate to the last put a flask of frozen orange juice next to her knockers to defrost. "I'm going down; don't care what you say."

She laughed a deep throaty masculine laugh. "Further down than you think, lover."

"Bye! I have had better sex with a llama." Months later, Algy's conscience worried him about this ungallant farewell, but for the moment he had other concerns besides manners unacceptable to the spinster ladies of Edinburgh. He stashed a rope and ice stakes for rappelling into his rucksack. Her sneering laugh stayed with him as he walked to the cliff edge, and even as he hammered in a stake into the hard blue ice and abseiled to the foot of the buttress, where he had noticed an easy gully, which would take him up bypassing the first difficulties of the ridge. He pulled down the rope and stomped heavily towards the next drop off, hammered in another stake, and cut grooves below it to simulate a rope under pressure slicing the snow. Attaching the spare rope through the stake, he let it slither down till the ends touched the next landing, to look as if he had rappelled down. Meanwhile there were some amiably angled snow free rocks up the middle of the gully up which he scrambled leaving no trace of upward movement.

The gully turned a corner; without warning the rock reared up steeply. There was serious climbing ahead. Nothing daunted Algy moved steadily upwards on steep snow, which being in the shade remained reassuringly solid. In the steady rhythm of stab and kick, he began enjoying himself. His lungs were clear and he could feel a joyful surge of energy and well being. For the first time on the expedition he felt in command of his destiny. Around him were the stupendous peaks of the Cordillera Blanca. A huge bird, a condor surely, swooped and swerved around him, then hovered directly above him as if showing the way. The gully ended in a tremendous rock *cul-de-sac*. The bird settled on a rock up to the right, flapped its wings and cawed invitingly. He traversed across a steep discontinuous band of ice towards the bird. The exposure was tremendous, but Algy was elated and gloried in it. Above him was a broken buttress. There was no going back. Up he went following the bird, hopping from rock to rock. Threading his way precisely after the condor, who he decided to call Ariadne, he found no harder than Curved Ridge on the Buchaille in Glencoe, steep but blessed with solid incuts that seemed to turn up on command. On it went. Algy felt victorious, happy and glorious. Destiny had provided him with this moment; he wasn't going to let it down.

Algy's elation took a dip when he was confronted with a vertical blank wall, and the sun took this moment to disappear behind a cloud. A sudden chill on the rock was transmitted to Algy. He shivered as if someone had stepped on his grave, and then nervously traversed to the left to face a short steep ice wall that petered out into a tricky little ice gully. Tussling with it gave him back his confidence. A light golden mist through which the sun was trying to break through surrounded him. The gully now was furnished with fine rocky steps that put him atop a pinnacle. He sat there with nowhere to go, but no worries. He broke off a chunk of Kendal Mint Cake. Fluff from his pocket stuck to the sweet like flypaper. Some things don't change. He smiled.

The bird, he really couldn't tell a condor from an albatross, had settled in a large basin of rock maybe 80ft down and across a gap. It cawed and waved at him. Algy uncoiled his rappel rope, found an anchor and slid down. Just before he landed the bird took off. Algy realized he was in a trap. Had Ariadne been leading him on? He made a mental note to consult the Rhyme of the Ancient Mariner. Then crossed that off his to do list, as he realized he had to survive first. He didn't pull down the rope in case he had to prussik his way out; something he didn't really relish. Ariadne was fluttering away down and to his left. With almost oriental fatalism, Algy penduled to the left, slid down and took up the perch, which the condor had obligingly just vacated.

Above was a slab thinly smeared with verglas. He tapped at the ice with his picks. They went in a millimeter and seemed to hold. No way could he kick with his crampons. The flimsy film would collapse. He tiptoed up with his crampons hanging on by a hair. If this pitch had been on the Ben, he knew he could never tackle it. Here on the High Andes far from ropes, belays and CIC Hut he went at it with a tremendous feeling of exhilaration. He was teetering on top of the world. He could only fall and die, or live to tell the tale. Life was seldom so simple.

A short whale back of snow led to a steepening and sharpening of the arête, till it became a filigree of ice. It occurred to him crossing this slender fin of ice, that he really was a roisterer, a rogue, and a devil may care rascal. Who should be his exemplar? Why not Errol Flynn? He tied a colored bandanna round his neck to give him the requisite jaunty swagger. In his pre-roistering days, he would have timorously ridden this ridge *a cheval* bumping his bottom along, but now he gaily tiptoed across this fine tightrope of ice, using his axe not for balance but for punching holes in the ice so that this diaphanous filigree resembled perforated paper. Unbeckoned, a remark heard in his green youth of Errol Flynn's 17 inches of uncontrollable flesh flashed before his mind's eye. Not having the faintest idea what it meant at the time he had ignored the inopportune lout who made it, but now he worried if he could measure up to his beau ideal. A moment's inattention. Whoosh! His foot slipped. The other one followed. He was hurtling down the slope. He slammed his axe into the ice; sparks flew between the ice and the steel. He threw his body on top of the axe, and slewed to a halt, his knees ripped raw by the friction of the ice. He gasped, his breath knocked out of him. If he made a sudden movement he would slide again this time with no hope of stopping. Carefully and painfully, for the abyss below him was suddenly frightening, he slogged his way back to the ridge hammering his axe deep into the ice at each step. His brow was cascading sweat, for it had been a damned near run thing. The rest of the ridge was traversed tight-lipped, less roisterously.

Ahead was a huge leaning buttress, obviously the crux. Algy was gasping for breath. It must be the altitude, but he suspected fear played its part. Surveying the rock tower ahead, he made out a line of disjointed cracks searing the right hand face of buttress. This had to be the way. Ariadne tipped her wing at it as if confirming his route choice. He took a swig of Gatorade. Gad, he should have told the waiter to take it back. Chewing off a slice of power bar almost broke his teeth. The bitter taste, no better than it should have been, brought to mind all his feelings about Cynthia. He was damned if he was going to die to oblige her.

He attacked the crack system; the tilt of the mountain's geology had fitted it with solid jugs. The climbing would have rated a mild Diff in the Lake District. Then it turned a corner. Without warning the crack reared to the vertical. He was half way through a casual swing to the right when he realized he was caught off balance, and unable to reverse the move. He knew his arm strength would give out very soon. He made a wild move up. Luckily his hand chanced to land on a big solid jug. Now he was faced with a ferocious unremitting layback. He hauled his way up, sliding his screaming arms up the sharp corner, legs braced and shuffling up against the opposite wall. But what with being hurriedly placed they were slipping slithering, and shaking uncontrollably! He screamed an inaudible prayer. On his harness hung a small Camelot. Why it was there he couldn't remember, but slapped it anyway into the overhanging crack, and clipped on. Take a chance. He dropped his weight on it. It held. He unslung his ice axe and skewered it into the crack higher up, then wound the rope round and hauled with all his might. Up he went, and with the weight coming off the camming device, it slipped out of the crack. He grabbed at the

Camelot and despite his fingers ripped painfully raw, bleeding from the rough granite managed to slot it in higher up. He wound the rope tightly a couple of turns round the axe; rested, then torquing the axe higher in the crack, he repeated the maneuver. Again and again he did the same till the crack began to lean back and the cliff took on a less ferocious aspect. He was glad none of his comrades had seen him cheating. But "Sometimes it is too high for ethics." He quoted Sir Christian Bonnington to himself. Ariadne, who had disappeared for a while, sat down beside him looking very pleased with herself, and squawked, "Hear, Hear!"

Algy was happy. He knew he had made it, even though he was more knackered than he knew what to do with. The clouds dropped below him. Above were the blue sky and the antipodean sun. The thick cotton wool layer below separated him from the tiresome world of mortals. Not far above, he glimpsed another fat brown rock glowing like a biscuit in its little bit of sunshine. No four star hotel could be more welcome. He sat down on the rock and relished the view. The bird was squawking and flapping its wings above him on another softer boulder. He was tired and sat there longer than he should. A chilling breeze told him to go on. From there was an easy slope to the summit. Waiting for him there was his feathered friend.

Two other climbers were sitting by the summit munching their hill butties. "Leave a crust for Ariadne," said Algy. They looked at him strangely. Meanwhile the bird was fluttering madly as if she wanted to tell him something. She flew up 20ft gave another caw, a flutter, and off she went. Algy who knew he would never see her again, waved his bandanna, "Ta, Ariadne. Theseus was a cad and a rotter." He knew what Ariadne was trying to tell him. Life was not something you learned at school, nor was it the best trophy house on the block. It came at you like a buffet on the wind. Seize it and you would be akin to the gods. Fluff and you might as well live in a shopping mall. However, the two climbers were still looking at him as if he were deranged, but not because of the man bird conversation. "Did you come up from there?" They pointed to his footprints leading back to the abyss. He nodded. "Where's your partner?" He shook his head. "Do you realize you have just made the first ascent of the Great Pillar of Huascaran, the greatest unclimbed challenge in the Andes?" There was nothing they couldn't do for him. Algy had quite a struggle to stop them carrying him down the mountain. For a brief spell he became the toast of Peruvian climbing circles, whose TV networks were surprised to find how camera shy he was.

He need not have been. Cynthia decided to short-circuit all her problems by murdering her authentic husband. She got careless, but a good attorney, and a lucrative plea agreement saw her all right. She is now doing 20 to life in Lucasville, Ohio, and is weaving the most gorgeous American Quilt, depicting her youthful adventures for her grandchildren. As yet she doesn't even have any children, but has a truly American sense of optimism.

Afraid of his own Shade

'Gordon Bennett!' Sidney Sharpeham clutched the steering wheel like he wanted to strangle it. 'Why does it have to play up now?'

The car juddered, and then revived throatily before optimistically leaping into full throttle. Aided by a billowing black cloud, the curtain was swiftly dropping on the day. It was late afternoon in bleak February, and Sidney had one last call to make. 'Please let me get this one in!' He muttered to the dashboard. He hated going to Grimsthorpe's mega-market. The man was rude, nasty rude, and always on the scrounge for sweeteners. The only way Sidney could get his toiletries on display was to outdo his competitors' bribes, for as Grimsthorpe delighted to point out, he had them by the short and curlies. One of his favorite frolics was to inspect the shelves carefully set up by the reps, and if the stacks didn't meet his military standards of precision he kicked the displays down. The ignorant sod had the little corporal complex; the little man used to being kicked around now getting the chance to put the boot in.

'Please, let me get this over with.' If he could endure what passed for Grimsthorpe's wit and get away quickly, he would have time to down a swift half with his mate, Albert before returning home. The engine gave an unhealthy cough, chuntered a couple of times, and then died. He knew what to do, done it many times before. There was this little wire, attached to the thingy-me-bob, which was stuck under the what-do-you-call-it that needed splicing. Just a few minutes ferreting about in the entrails of the motor and he would be on the road again.

Trouble was when he lifted the bonnet, it was pitch dark, and he couldn't for the love of Mike remember whether the thing-me-bob was on the left or on the right. 'At least I'm a wise virgin; I've got a lantern.' But when he took the torch out of the boot, the cold had killed the battery. Little flecks of wet snow pitter-pattering against the windows forced him back in the car. No sense in adding to his troubles by getting frostbite. The visit to Grimsthorpe's mega-mart was up the Swannee for a start, and he didn't fancy sitting the night out in the freezing car. There must be some habitation nearby. He gingerly opened the passenger side window an inch. Sure enough there was a light maybe two hundred yards down the lane from where he had stopped.

Almost as soon as he had stepped out of the car, he began to have second thoughts about the journey he had so blithely undertaken. He recalled a chastening experience as a youth, when he rashly bet his pals he could swim to an island in the middle of a black Scottish loch. It didn't seem very far at the time, but no sooner had he hit the water than the island receded into the distance, and at every bone chilling stroke moved further away. Now he was back in that loch, except it was this mucky lane, and the light kept on retreating, till he wondered if it was a star, light years away. His mind was playing all sorts of games with him. Had one of his mates spiked his lunchtime pint?

'I wish I'd put a coat on for this hike.' Sid was no outdoorsman. On the muddy trek in the pitch dark his city shoes were useless. He skidded on the brink of an icy puddle just managing not to fall in. There was an old fifties banger in surprisingly good nick and an antique horse plow parked on either side of a rustic front door, like guardians of the gate. He reached the door and rapped on the grinning lion knocker. 'Please, please, answer the door.' He hopped about from foot to foot to stop shivering. After what felt like a long interval, a very frightened young girl cautiously opened the door. 'What do you want?' She said none too friendly. Sidney had not been salesman of the year for nothing. No problem here, he thought, so on went the patter backed up by the sincere smile that had sold a million toilet rolls. 'Look. I know this is an intrusion, awfully inconvenient and the wrong time of day to come a-calling, but I'm in a spot of bother. If you wouldn't mind lending me a torch, it won't take a second to fix my car and I'll be out of your hair in no time.' The girl involuntarily, it seemed to Sidney, stroked her hair back off her neck with both her hands. Maybe she didn't realize it was a figure of speech, and he smiled again to soften the way for a further explanation. His smile did the business, for the tension in her shoulders visibly relaxed.

'Here! Come in out of the snow.' They moved into a dark paneled hall furnished with a nest of coats and a brass stand for walking sticks. An ancient melody was being ground out on an old gramophone. It was *Red Sails in the Sunset*. "Haven't heard that since I were a nipper." The girl just stood; her face expressionless. The salesman in him scouted around for something to break the silence between them. Under the stairs an old grandfather clock complete with pendulum chimed reassuringly, reminding Sidney Sharpeham of visits to his grandmother when he was a boy. 'Reminds me of visiting my granny when I was a lad.' The girl smiled, but showed no curiosity about his filial pilgrimages.

"Come into the best room." They went into one of those all purpose rooms that served as dining room, lounge, and place where you watched the telly. The girl pointed out a row of flying plaster ducks on the wall. "Them's Muriels," Sidney said, and the girl seemed to get the reference to Hilda Ogden on The Street for she smiled. Establish common ground, that was the reps first maxim. He gave the room the once over. Someone very old must live here. There were, could you believe it, lace doilies protecting the arms of the sofa and armchairs.

The girl had been fishing around at the bottom of a cupboard. An old broom, a faded remnant of carpet, and assorted fragments from a ping pong net were chucked out to form an untidy heap in the middle of the carpet.

'That ought to do you.' She handed him a torch of industrial proportions.

'Need a hand tidying up.'

'Nah it's easy.'

'Sure? Well Ta then. I'll be back in two shakes of a lamb's tail.'

'I'll have a cup of tea waiting.'

'Ah! I could murder a cuppa.'

'Them's fightin' words.'

The snow was coming down in increasing blasts riding on the tail of a bitter wind. Despite this he smiled to himself. The girl's last old-fashioned remark showed his knock 'em down charm was still fully operational. His district manager had always said his best assets were his open honest countenance and the easy smile that could melt the North Pole. But the open bluff face was a facade. In a tough market flogging bog rolls, Sid Sharpeham was as ruthless as they come.

True to his word he was back at the door in five minutes. The storm had shown no signs of abating and he was glad to be back in the warmth of the best room. Beside the cup of tea the girl had laid down a neat dram of whisky. Her education had not been entirely lacking.

'What's your line of work, then mister?' He told her, and she told him she went to a tech college in the local market town, which taught courses specially tailored for the sons and daughters of the soil. Sidney agreed that this was a better idea than wasting time on Integrated Studies and Sex Ed. which was all they seemed to do these days. Sydney wondered if he had somehow gone too far, for she looked at him curiously, then relaxed.

'See here, mister. I've got a steak and kidney pudding in the oven and a brickie's load of chips in the fryer. Why don't you help me eat them? You look half starved by the sight of you. Any road, if you don't they'll just go to waste.'

Sharpeham couldn't see the harm in that proposal. His schedule was now in disarray. Hurrying down the road had little appeal, and now he could legitimately put off the horrors of dealing with Grimsthorpe. Meanwhile the girl was an interesting study, intelligent possibly. There was no mad gleam in her eyes, so there was little chance she would go for him with the bread knife.

'Thank you kindly, my fair damosel, who cometh to my aid in time of distress.' Maybe he was laying it on too thick. The girl looked up suddenly to see if he was taking the mickey. It was the first time he had a good look at her. You wouldn't say she was beautiful. One eye was slightly off kilter, and the slight kink in the downhill slope of her nose eliminated her from the cannons of classical beauty. But she had dark hair with a raven's sheen to it, and dark eyes that came alive with an enigmatic smile, which seemed to say 'You don't know everything mister.' With the air of a connoisseur rating a fine wine, he reckoned her 'very bonny,' not quite the bon cru of a rare vintage, but you wouldn't kick her out of bed; the salesman's ultimate accolade.

'Me name's Griselda Ellis. What's your'n?' Sidney Sharpeham told a lie. Never give away anything except free samples; it was the salesman's absolute law.

'I expect you'd like some beer?'

"Is the pope a catholic?" Sid felt like the sailor home from the troubled sea. A couple of cans of Carlsberg Special later, Griselda was rabbitting on about something, but Sid wasn't paying much attention. He was doing calculations in his head. Not whether he was going to get it, but whether he was going to get away with it. In his salad days he had been a bit of a Jack the Lad, but now was another story. His wife had ways of extracting the truth the KGB would have been proud of. As for the penalty for straying, let's say he yearned for the Gulags.

'That storm's coming on wicked. You best consider staying the night?'

Griselda couldn't know that his look of indecision wasn't nerves, but came from a mental conflict between nostalgia for a lost lusty youth and middle aged common sense telling him to leave well alone.

'Listen, me duck. Me dad's in hospital; me mam's gone visiting him. They won't be back tonight. 'N me sister's out somewhere with her boyfriend. Lucky Cow! And *she* won't be coming home soon if that's what's worrying you.'

There was a familiarity about the structure of this scenario and a feeling that this was going down a preordained path, which made him faintly uneasy. Then it all began to click into place. He was in the middle of the classic Traveling Salesman Joke, of which he had heard so many variants so many times, in so many Friday lunchtime pubs. It went like this. There was this traveling salesman, see. His car breaks down in a lonely spot. He goes to lonely farmhouse for help. Only the farmer's daughter is at home. She offers him comfort and sustenance over and above requirements of hospitality. (A nod and a wink comes in handy here.) Some months later the salesman happens by the farm and makes a return visit, where the punch line is delivered. He knew that Carlsberg Special was strong but it had never before brought on hallucinations. Again he wondered if someone had popped something into his Marston's at lunchtime.

Griselda walked over to a revamped Juke Box, pressed some buttons and out came Pat Boone singing 'April Love,' a song he recognized from his school days. The wine-well it was beer- the woman, and song, all the old dangerous siren signals were coming together.

"Er, I think I'd better be off home now, but thanks very much for the offer. It's been a lovely evening, but I really have to press on, regardless."

"As the bishop said to the actress." She smiled, maybe ruefully. He couldn't think of a reply. "Yeah, rather. Well I'm off. Ta for everything." The trudge back to the car was horrible, up to his ankles in slush and ice, shoes leaking and socks soaking, he kept slithering and sliding, just about managing to stay upright. The car was encrusted with snow, capped by crystalline ice. He couldn't see the keyhole; never mind opening the door. Looking at the roads covered in a sheen of black ice and peppered with a fine covering of snow, he thought, driving is for fools tonight.

He went back to the house. God, how could he have considered going out? "I feel a bit of a twit, but would you mind if I reconsidered your kind offer. I mean you reconsidering. If it's still available that is." His teeth were chattering so much, he wondered, if she knew what he was saying.

"Confucius he say. 'That which is inevitable, lie back and enjoy.'" These archaic catch phrases she kept coming out with. Where did she get them from? A bad fifties joke book? Sidney wasn't irritated. His total attention was elsewhere. The slight misalignment of one eye now seemed an interesting feature, a Venerean Strabismus; that tell tale sign of mystic

121

allure. "Coom on in then." She had taken off her dress and was standing there in an ivory silk slip, which was doing a good job of emphasizing her vital statistics. 'Oops, seem to have a run in me nylons.' She lifted the lace hem up to her stocking tops. A very old fashioned girl she was. But Sid's mind was running on other things. That glimpse had settled it. As far as he was concerned it was a done deal.

The next morning there was no post-coital embarrassment as between brief encounters amongst strangers. "John Smith- that's the name of the man rescued by Hiawatha, aint it?" Sid, whose knowledge of American history was sketchy, said, 'Yep. That's me granddad.'

'Oh! John Smith, you are a proper caution, you are. What you need is a proper breakfast.' And a proper breakfast was what he was going to get. Starting with a large bowl of Grapenuts -By the bye Sidney found a lucky Grapenuts club badge in the packet, which he filched for his daughter. He was faintly surprised they still did that- they ploughed through the full Monty of bacon, eggs, sausages, tinned tomatoes and two slabs of fried bread to dunk with. Toast and marmalade, and a third cup of tea you could stand the spoon up in, and finally a fag, Capstan Full Strength, to ease the digestive process.

Outside the sun was beaming as if to catch up for lost time. The snow and ice had melted away, leaving a nice glossy sheen on the old paintwork. The storm, the last desperate throes of winter, was now a memory

'Come back again. I like you, really, really do like you, John Smith, even though you're older than me dad.' The car skidded away in the mud.

'Yeah, sure.' Sharpeham said to the dashboard. He was true to his professional ethic; love 'em and leave 'em. Anyway at that juncture he was more focused on putting together a convincing tale for Mrs. Sharpeham.

....

A year later, he was in the same area, and found himself drawn back to the house. He remembered the *dénouement* of the classic tale and smiled. As if? But what a story he would have for the lads. And what the heck? He needed a bit of an escape. Work had been rough. As far as the district manager was concerned, he had lost his shine, and the domestic front wasn't much of an improvement, what with his standards of husbandry being adversely critiqued by the missus.

The lane, which didn't seem as long as he remembered, had been black topped, so he could drive right up to the door. In the summer sunshine, the house seemed somehow neater. In place of the old banger, was a fairly new Honda Accord. The antique plowshare had also been removed, replaced by a yawning shaggy dog.

He rang the bell, which piped out in reply a jaunty chorus from Mamma Mia. Where was the grinning lion door-knocker? An elderly woman, presumably Griselda's mother, opened it cautiously. 'Yes?' The intonation was neutral, not terribly friendly. Sidney put a supreme effort into summoning up his smarmiest smile. 'Is Griselda home for visitors?'

'You, wot?' The daft old bat couldn't hear. And now the intonation, which had sprung up an octave was decidedly unfriendly. Patiently as if he was speaking to a deaf Zulu, Sidney enunciated, 'Griselda, Griselda Ellis. Is she in?' This seemed to have taken a good two minutes for completion, from delivery through reception to final dawning comprehension. The elderly woman's body convulsed as though she had been smacked on the head. 'Who the _____ are you?' He couldn't hear the precise expletive for she had slammed the door at the moment of utterance, but the message was clear. He stood gazing at the door like he was expecting a replay with a better outcome. It took a lot to deflate Sharpeham, but this encounter knocked the stuffing out of him. He retreated to his car baffled and shaken. Even in defeat he retained a smidgeon of his winning ways, for the woman seeing the slump in his shoulders took him for an honest man, and rushed out of the house, her entire body fat wobbling in time, with her rushing stride. 'Young man, wait!' Young man-well that was a start in the right direction. The old girl was puffing and panting from the unaccustomed exertion. 'Who gave you that name?' Sensing danger Sharpeham prevaricated. 'Bloke in the Local gave me to understand someone of that name lived here.' He gave her his so innocent, 'What me?' look, the one he used as a last line of defense against irate store managers.

'You gave me quite a turn, me lad. Tell you what. Come inside, and 'ave a cuppa. We can have a right good natter, over nowt or owt.'

They went inside. "Come sit ye down, lad. Make thisself at home."

The room had been redone, like it was saying welcome to the twenty-first century. She had already settled a plateful of Bakewell Tarts on him and was swishing hot water round the tea-pot to warm it, when she said, 'It was forty years ago, I think. Me sister were called Griselda, Griselda Ellis, like you said. She were young 'bout eighteen, a bonny lass, the sort everyone takes to. Honest as the day is long, but too honest if you know what I mean. She trusted people, people you wouldn't give time of day to. She knew house were haunted. There were stories. Lots. Not headless ladies, but peculiar things you couldn't put down to anything normal. Like sightings of people when there weren't nobody 'round. But she weren't fazed. She thought everyone were friendly, even ghosts. We were all out the night she went away in her mind. It were like her wits went up in smoke, or her head spirited away by fairies. It were February. I remember like it were yesterday. There was a freak storm that night, winter's last blast, when a distressed stranger came to the door, so she said, a traveling man, dressed peculiar like, who vanished next day." She shook her head sadly. "Of course there weren't nobody. No one else saw him come or go.

There were no foot tracks, no car tracks, and our lane was right muddy then. No one heard any car, and they usually do. They are a right nosy bunch round her, always peeping out of curtains, and minding other folks business more than their own.

"It was pure fancy, the whole thing. Her gran used to tell stories of a servant girl in the reign of good king Charles, not the one as had his head taken off the other one with the spaniels, as had a ghostly lover. She was obsessed with story. Mind you there's little enough to occupy your mind round here, so she dreamt it all up for want of anything better to do. She became besotted with her traveling man, totally doolally." Her index finger made a stirring motion beside her temple as illustration. "Used to go out every night crying after her lost love. There were nowt we could do with her. Me mam couldn't take any more of her and her weary crazy affliction, so we had to parcel her off to the funny farm. The lass were that bad at first they locked her up in padded cell. They tried electric shock treatment, and pills. She must of swallowed a lorry load of them. Course nothing worked. Then along came Maggie Thatcher. You know the rest. She closed all the loony bins and dumped all of them poor souls, mad, bad and sad back on their families. Community treatment, they called it; sweeping under carpet, I say."

She paused, to wipe a tear off her reddened face. Recalling all of this made her sad. Then as if coming back to the present she said, "What did you say your name was?" Sidney Sharpeham lied again. 'Well you're here; you may as well see her.' Sidney sat bolt upright. The old girl said, 'You do want to see her? You who've come a hunting for her. She's upstairs, you know. Let me just call up to her; see if she's presentable.'

Sidney Sharpeham had to put down his cup of tea. His trembling hands set up a storm in the teacup so violent the wavelets threatened to overflow and soak the table-cloth.

'Grizzly, there's a gent dahn 'ere as wants to see you.'

'Tell 'im to bugger off!' There was a faint echo of the voice he remembered, but the timbre was swallowed up in wheezing and coughing, as a beautiful Roman gold coin might, having been encrusted with the mould of uncounted centuries.

'Says his name is 'John Smith.'' There was a pause. Sidney heard in the background the clock strike whatever hour it was, then a long drawn out demented squeal.

'My John, me darlin' John! I knew you'd come! Hold on! Wait till I get's me sticks. Me knees are playing me up some'at awful. I will be down in two shakes of a lamb's tail.'

Sid Sharpeham was out the door into his car in no time, and drove off skidding from side to side over the tarmac as if it were mud. A little way down the road he was pulled over for reckless driving.

Tiptoe through the Treetops

During lunchtime all the instructors left the site. To be fair most of the others had already called in, pleading sickness that morning or discovering that they had other pressing engagements as soon as they found out that "that" school was coming to visit the adventure center. Grandparents long since laid to rest were hastily re-interred that day. A handful of staff acting above and beyond the call of duty and reason, grimly hung on until the mid-day break. Then they formed a deputation, and told their leader in no uncertain terms, enough was enough.

In spite of the Australian Bush hat, aggressively florid beard and deer-hunting knife the chief-instructor was quite a mild-mannered chap, a Mr. Pickwick of the Great Outdoors. At the moment he was shouting at the teacher-in-charge. "Get the Hell out of here," his fat jolly chins quivered in fury as he tore up the contract, "Never bring these little asswipes near this camp again!" There was an exultation in his voice and bearing. He knew his words would get him into hot water with educators everywhere. He didn't care. He felt a sense of power, a brief spell of being Patrick Henry, cutting adrift the anchor of conventional allegiance.

The group leader, a faded 30-somethinger with a permanent look of being in need of a stiff drink, took the sentence of banishment in her stride. Munching on an overstuffed ham and cheese bun, she nodded solemnly. She had long accepted her school's role as the pariah of the great city of Americus' Educational Establishment, and was quite used to summary expulsion from whatever Garden of Eden they had managed to wangle their way into, so that she had become quite a dab hand at whistling up transport at very short notice to return the little thuglets to the barricaded barrack-block they called school.

"Right, you guys," she bawled in a surprisingly powerful voice," clear up your trash and let's hit the road." Bread pellets and salami shrapnel, all of which managed to travel an impressive distance, peppered this announcement.

"Aw no, miz Peabody. Why we gotta go?" those within hearing distance called out. The kids had been enjoying themselves, and like most badly disciplined children had no concept of how naughty they really were. To their teachers, however, who had been sitting around in little disconsolate huddles warding off the forays of the stinging bees attracted by the piles of rejected food, big enough to provide a modest Third World Village for a week, the announcement of the dismissal came as no surprise, and was only tinctured by a little annoyance that they would be deprived of their post-prandial smoke, while their charges were off pillaging the environment.

The children, hovering around about the tables, could be immediately categorized as the tubbier of the group, and had been kept in earshot by the attraction of the dull, dry, packed lunch, that would never offer a challenge to the burger emporia, which were such a feature of their daily lives and where eventually all their career paths would run. On reception of the command to pack up, they began running around in pointless circles bawling and throwing sandwich fragments at each other. The staff started bellowing, "C'mon, you guys," almost like a reprise, a choral echo to their now energized leader. The kids took not a blind bit of notice. No one was surprised. Anyway they all liked to shout a bit. The teachers when they emerged from their daily maelstrom had to make a conscious effort to down-tone a vast number of decibels to retain domestic harmony, while the fat kids screamed louder at home, a hopeless effort since they were competing for affection with several cable channels.

Meanwhile the children's more free-spirited brethren were further afield busily vandalizing the trees and the safety conscious adventure equipment, which lay in their branches. It was their final project, an attempt to raise a forest fire, which had stoked the chief instructor's wrath.

If only anybody knew it, their actions were quite in keeping with the spirit of the savage Indians, who two hundred years ago had roamed around this area and given a hard time to the early pioneers in this part of Ohio. They were a far different kettle of fish from the Native Americans dreamt up by the purveyors of late twentieth century sensibilities. Those gentle woodland ghosts making beads, eating berries and carving out boring, inarticulate artifacts and living in harmony with the forces of nature had long before the coming of the rude boisterous schoolchildren been driven westwards to extinction.

Young Timmy was perhaps the last survivor of that tribe of innocents. His little group of fourteen year olds had wandered so far into the forest that they were beyond recall. The bawling so ear splitting at point-blank range was reduced at this part of the woods to a gentle soughing through the leaves overhead inseparable from other forest sounds. Like a glacial erratic his forebears had been left high and dry when their tribal cousins had retreated from a sterner human climate. He too had accepted his lot. He was far too gentle and refined to be taken on as a member of the hooligan gang. Used to being ignored and bullied he had given up jumping up to make people take notice or shouting to be heard. The way he spoke was much too grammatical to be interesting, and so he had reached the dismal state where his friends were too bored with him to beat him up. Let's face it he was just plain uncool.

But now he was having his day. He took to the "Tree Tops " high ropes circuit like an ardent squirrel. He scrambled up the castaways net, romped over the commando crawl and leapt fearlessly at the Tarzan Swing. "Look at me!" he yelled launching himself at a really far away tree and for the first time they looked at him and not without respect, for the only virtue that mattered to bad boys was courage and Timmy had that quality in abundance. Twyler and Ned, elected leaders on account of their unsurpassed malice, had to admit that Timmy's courage outstripped by far their naughtiest exploit, slashing the tires of their least favorite teacher and pouring half a pound of sugar into his gas-tank.

Twyler and Ned's screaming and tumbling in the net appeared pathetic beside Timmy's flying through the air with the greatest of ease, that daring young man on the flying trapeze. Carrie looked at them with ill-concealed contempt as she masticated her gum, and her eyes, when she turned to Timmy shone with the kind of sheen that had hitherto been reserved for the school's star quarterback, on whom she had an enormous crush.

For a long time Timmy had been madly in love with Carrie with the hopeless passion of the social reject with no scale of reference on which to base his possible chances, and so unstoked but unquenched, his unrequited infatuation had burst into a passionate flame, with the result that he was unable to eat the tasteless school lunches he was faced with every day. Macaroni and cheese pizzas had turned to their pre-micro-waved collection of dried up chemicals in his mouth, while he gazed at Carrie placidly munching the school swill, her lunchtime gum stuck under the table for the interim to preserve the flavor. An outside observer might be disconcerted by the flinty fixity of her gaze, too strong, too knowing in one so young, but now she was making sheep's eyes at him. Her jaws chewed relentlessly as usual, but the movement was purely mechanical; her heart was not in it. All of a sudden he saw her and being a quick-witted lad tutored by the afternoon soaps, recognized what had transformed from a thousand scenarios. She had taken a fancy to him. His stomach did a quick jump and he almost fell off his perch, saved only by the quick reactions of Twyler and Ned, who grabbed him and saved him from being entombed in the leaf mould twenty feet below.

"Timmy, Oah my Gaad! You're like so .....!" Carrie's powers of articulation gave out, but it was an avowal as heartfelt as anything uttered by Keats or Coleridge. Even though she finished off limply with an "so oh cool," Timmy knew he made a conquest and even at that early innocent stage in his life, realized with a fleeting pang that he had attained a pinnacle of bliss, that even if he lived to be a hundred, his life would never match.

"Strike now, Timmy," his inner voice told him, "while the iron is still hot." This wisdom was supplied by a recent episode of Guiding Light. In the world of soaps, female affections changed as rapidly as the tunes on their I-pods. Perhaps subconsciously he had mastered that lesson and saw that to seal the compact he needed to create a *coupe de foudre*. He shrugged, "Easy Pie, I can do this blindfold." Carrie's eyes shone with a watery metallic sheen and her gum went down her throat. "Give me that as a blindfold." Timmy pointed to the spare tee casually slung around her shoulders. "Tie it on for me, will you, Carrie?" It was a command not a question, but the change in tone went unnoticed in the little group crowding around Timmy admiringly. Self-consciously with a touch of proprietorial pride, Carrie's hands shook as she tied on the blindfold, emblazoned with Treetops motto, "Trust is a five letter word." An unfamiliar jolt, frightening and excruciatingly exquisite passed through

Timmy's stomach, when he felt the little crab apples of Carrie's incipient bosoms airbrush his cheeks. In his sightlessness, he recalled a teacher in the nice school he used to attend telling the class about King Arthur's Court and how the ladies would give their betrothed knights a favor such as a handkerchief before they went into battle. This fanciful memory evoking chivalry, hobgoblins and towers fantastically adorned with embattlements and gryphons, excited him far more than the first shoots of physical lust, which he had just experienced. Poor Timmy, alas, there was no romantic echo in the bosom of his ladylove. Her formative years had not been passed in the company of Tennyson, Mallory, or Geoffrey of Monmouth or anyone, owning even an abridged version of the code of chivalry. The canon, she adhered to, from which she drew moral sustenance, was the jungle etiquette of the internet. Gunfire and violence supplied the answers to any moral questions. No poetry flowed through her veins only the verbal sewage of the kind inescapable in this genre.

"Wow!" Carrie applauded as he gingerly felt his way over the panther crawl. "Way cool!" his newfound admirers muttered, throwing superlatives out in gay abandon. High above them Timmy could almost feel their tremulousness, but he himself felt no fear in his heart, slewing his way over the commando crawl. Blinded but undeterred he romped the course. There was one last thing he had to do. He had no fear for himself and his own ability. Did he trust his newly established friends? If he could do that he would have conquered fear itself, and he remembered Jake in "Peebles Plaza" saying to the wayward but delectable Melbourne, " Fail to Trust; fail to love." She had failed the trust test and was thereupon ditched, a moral for all the myriads of impressionable viewers, who gained their education from the tube.

" I am going to do the zip line- blind." He could hear them muttering down below "The zip line!" "Twyler, Ned, you fix me to the pulley. Carrie, come up here. Stand by me and launch me off.

It took quite a while to arrange, as they had to clamber over several obstacles to reach him. They weren't very fast. Indeed they were surprisingly timid. He waited patiently, till at last they were up beside him, thrashing and struggling on the swaying ropes. He could sense their anxiety through the layers of the blindfold. It dropped over his nose and mouth and sticking his tongue into its folds he could catch an inkling of her sweet body odor. They began fiddling clumsily with the ropes; breathing heavily, not cool at all. A hand went round his neck stroking it, caressing him. It must have been Carrie since she was by his side, whispering coyly in his ear," I'm putting a note in your pocket. Read it afterwards." "What does it say?" he croaked, his voice cracking with the excitement. "Wait and see," she giggled and touched him on the nose He could taste her sweet cloying perfume in his mouth. In his enraptured mood he thought of it as his first kiss. The hand that went into his pocket strayed slowly over the front of his trousers. Spasms coruscated from his loins to tingle in his hair and in his toes. There was a gentle push to help him on his way, and he had the sweetest most penetrating orgasm of his short life.

That night the temperature dropped with the sudden jolt that is usual at that time of year in Ohio. Riding hard on the skirts of the frigid front came a vast black storm cloud traveling across the innermost counties of the state like a great armed horde from some ancient biblical epic. The blizzard took over the night covering all tracks in an impeccable shining white blanket, and people woke up to the surprising sight of snow weighing down the still leafy trees, enhancing the brilliant fall colors, so that it looked as if crimson stains had been sputtered over pristine white bed linen. It was as though the whole of Ohio had been the setting for a very gory version of MacBeth.

The hunters were the first to discover the hanged boy, swinging stiffly, the rope creaking with the breeze. A forlorn stiff T-shirt was located not far from the boy by the hunters. The police had no difficulty in dismissing it as evidence in the case. Forensic identified it as a girl's garment and the boy had never been near a girl as the suicide note in his pocket indicated. The pathetic scrap of paper spoke of a loner, who couldn't make any friends and had done away with himself when the object of his only human feeling hardly knew he existed. There had been a rash of juvenile suicides in the area. Several educational conferences had been convened to discuss the phenomenon. The favorite settings for these last desperate acts were school lavatories. Timmy's case was interesting only because of its arboreal backdrop, but the fact that really perked up the educational social workers was that the victim was part Native American. A blizzard of learned papers followed fast on the heels of the real storm.

The Garden Gnome

Of course it was a rock. The movement of the light riding the escarpment would recast it in its base form within the hour, but in this fleeting moment the due process of wind, rain and snow coupled with thunderous rumblings from the bowels of the earth had hewn this replica of an old Indian. This was not in itself remarkable. Dotted around the wilder parts of Ohio were bevies of them, from the rocks above Lancaster where Chief Tarhe gazes down stonily at the Sunday traffic, to Old Man's Cave, with its sphinx indifferently observing the masses swarming about the rock pool at the trail's end. A little poking around had to be added to imagination to find the right spot to support the image. But from wherever you peeked at this bit of Nature's sculpture, there was no mistaking the Mongoloid features of the Native American. Except, this one was smoking. Two creamy profiteroles of smoke floated up to spot the blue sky behind his head.

It was a spring day in the Zaleski Forest. Normally he came here in dreary November for the solitude of the silent woods under gray skies, but today the air was crisp with that undefined feeling of anticipation sprouting with the green shoots of reawakening life. Over-head a hawk settled on a branch creaking under its new burden of leaves; red-winged blackbirds followed the path chirping continuously, and in a tree close by a piliated woodpecker was tapping out happy thoughts. Strewn about his feet, were lavender, mauve, violet, and even some blooms that could have passed for the bonny bluebells of Scotland, a whole array of pastel colored flowers unfurled on a Pre-Raphaelite landscape.

The contrast between the melancholy forest, he knew, and this multi-colored extravaganza touched off a sensory explosion that knocked his perceptions out of joint. Maybe he was merely faint with hunger, for he was unfit, had pushed himself a bit hard, and his hurried breakfast was hours ago. Now here was this curious figure on the skyline, still smoking! The hiker had to go up and take a closer look. Just as he started up, another little cluster of puffballs sent up smoke signals into the otherwise immaculate blue sky.

The rock was odd, chocolate brown, out of place, surrounded by the normal Appalachian grey stone. The way ahead, steep and tangled with roots, called for care, so it wasn't till the man got there, that he noticed the sculpture had swiveled from profile to directly head on. Had he been drinking last night, he asked himself? No, leastways no more than usual. Then unmistakably *it* or should one say 'he' moved, proffering a stick the man recognized, from the Westerns Channel as a pipe of peace. Holding the bowl, he shook the pipe stem slightly to indicate that it was the hiker's turn for a smoke. Without quite knowing why the hiker took the pipe, had a quick glance at the stem and began to smoke

Puffing away at the calumet, he let the stone man examine his pack, which was crammed with all the tools of the modern frontiersman, camera, watch, altimeter, map and compass. He hadn't surrendered so totally to high tech that he needed a GPS for a ramble in the Hocking, but it had been touch and go whether to bring a cell phone. The stranger tapped each item in turn all the while shaking his head like it was bad medicine. He looked at the white man, and pointed to the sky, as if saying "Why? You have the sun for direction." He pointed to a tree, indicating the moss encircling the northern side of the bark. The man got the point. If there is no sun, read the moss on the tree as a compass. Then the Indian pointed at his feet indicating follow me.

The native led the white man along the crest of the ridge, the one gliding, the other crashing and slithering through the undergrowth. He put a finger to his lips and smiled. It was an unusual smile like the crinkling of old leather. And then with ne'er a snap, crackle or pop, he padded over a crunchy mass of last year's leaves.

Down paths the white man never suspected existed, the Indian led him, pointing out the haunts of bear, bobcat and wolf, creatures, that by all accounts had been cleared out way, way, back. Then very quickly the Indian strung an arrow, pointed the bow, but the arrow never took flight. "Why don't you shoot?" Said the other in a forced, frozen whisper. He could have sworn a bear was staring at them from a bush not a yard and a half away. A brute bear in Southern Ohio? The red man shook his head, and made a sign like gentle waves breaking on the lake saying, "There is no danger" while the bear rumbled amiably past. His hand made a curve over the white man's stomach meaning, "There is too much meat, even for you, big beef eater. What we don't need, we leave, and so do not deplete the forest."

The odd couple strolled along the sandy fringe of a meandering stream. Something was wrong. A second later it clicked. The water was clean, the banks, and meadows were totally devoid of beer cans or fast-food remnants. The Native American shoved his hand in the water, poked about for a bit and came up guddling a trout like an old Scots poacher. After sparking a flint at a mini-tepee of tinder and sticks, the old Indian soon had the trout sizzling over the flames. The city man lay basking in the sun, as though he had lived all his life in the forest, smacking his lips over a fish, that couldn't have been bettered at the best fish restaurant in Columbus.

Well satisfied, they ambled down into Furnace Hollow. At least it looked like the Hollow, but with the furnace, road and parking lot taken out. Following an ancient hunting trail by the river, the strange man pointed at the ground and then his feet, meaning, "Disturb nothing, leave no trace. Only what is here stays here." His arm swept high to embrace all their surroundings, and then pointed specifically at himself clearly saying, "The Shawnee lives in harmony with this." The white man cast his eyes around at the pristine woodland. Where were the rusty washing machines, the clapped out engine parts, the miscellaneous garbage which normally furnished this patch of the Buckeye State? All gone. The forest was more beautiful, far more beautiful, than he remembered, and the sky was as clear as on a mountaintop.

A tissue fell out of the hiker's pocket, at once the Indian pounced on this, handed it back forcibly, then passed his finger across his throat in an unmistakable gesture.

There was more from the Native American on the lines that the Great Spirit despoils the despoiler of the earth. Although he leavened every silent sermon with chuckles to round off every *caveat*, he left no doubt about the consequences of unsound woodland practices. The traveler wondered how the woodsman would regard real estate developers, shopping mall builders and other serious despoilers of Nature. If the Indian had his way bad medicine would be coming down the pike for them, and they would be struck down, purple-faced on the golf green-their last stroke, that big birdie in the sky, a vulture.

The interval for digestion over, they moved onto dessert, wild strawberries, and blueberries, eased down with a generous dash of tizwaz, which he privately reckoned not quite up to his wife's margaritas, but devastating in its own way. What a perfect finish to a splendid day, he thought, lazing on the downy heather, before slipping into a delightful doze.

He woke up, head pounding and dizzy. Too much tizwaz, or maybe exposure to the sun, he couldn't be sure. Taking stock of his surroundings, he saw that he was back at the rock, now just another stony lump resembling nothing much else. There was no Indian, no pipe of peace, just birds chirruping on the park trail below, and trees dancing in a heat haze. Had it all been a dream? If so, it was an odd one, without scene or cast changes, and a story line that held firm from curtain-up to down. Also it was a moral tale, and he had never before had a dream where right and wrong affected the narrative.

Driving home through the byways of Hocking County he couldn't bring himself to turn on the radio, so caught up was he by the spell of his dream. Finally at home, when he lifted his gear out of the car the hiker noticed the garden gnome sitting on top of the tree stump in his yard. It was one of his life's familiar landmarks, so familiar he never bothered looking at it. Unusually for one of his plastic tribe, this one was beardless and uncapped, defects that got him thrown in as a freebie, along with a job lot of normal gnomes at the garden center. Being the odd gnome out, the hiker felt sorry for him, and the hatless dwarf rapidly became his favorite. He stuck the little fellow on top of the rockery and forgot about him.

What now really caught his eye was that the gnome was the spitting image of his Indian. Tuck him up in a hillside on a warm spring day and they would be as like as Tweedledum and Tweedledee. He shrugged his shoulders, and went indoors. So it was a dream, a dream concocted from a piece of forgotten furniture. He resolved to be a bit more careful with the sauce on a Friday night before a hike in the hills.

That evening after dinner he and his wife sat outside nursing their glasses of wine, watching the sun setting on the rockery and the gnome glowing with a splendid copper fire, when he told her about his unusual day.

"I mean, why did it happen to me, Heather? If I had been back-hoeing out farmland to stick a Wal-Mart here, a Kroger there, the old Indian's lecture would have come in handy. But why choose a middle of the road grade-school teacher, who even picks up his kids' trash after every lesson? Everything the Chief showed me on the picnic I agreed with already, so what's the point? Mmm!"

"I don't know, Jim? But look at the expression on Grumpy's face. What do you reckon to it? It's, it's like ...." Heather, also a teacher, taught social studies and was seldom at a loss for a parallel from the past. "What does he look like, so pleased with himself? Like he was Sitting Bull the morning after Custer's Last Stand."

Jim laughed, "Funny you saying that. But, seeing it in this light you might be right about the facial expression."

"Had you noticed it before?"

"No, never. I always thought of him as a humble gnome."

"More of your common or garden gnome?"

He laughed again. Heather always got the last laugh.

"Cheers!"

"Cheers!"

But coming home late after another trip he got his answer. Over Lake Hope, the moon was gliding through the clouds, casting its reflection over the unruffled waters, like Salome slipping off her Seven Veils. For a moment, a picture was set out in front of him of such beauty that his heart ached with melancholy. He asked himself how long this would remain untouched. If he was honest he had to admit it wasn't only the developers who despoiled the wilderness. They were merely at the forefront. Everyone was an accessory, himself included. Even to that time, when in an unspoiled Eden, Caribs stood silently watching the Santa Maria scraping through sand and shingle onto their beach; and a young Columbus planted his feet securely onto a hemisphere of prime real estate.

The Marquis of Kettlewell

It was the end of an in Ibizan mini-break, and I was recovering somewhere in the ten deep mob thronging the check-in, when to the fore burst a tubby little man, florid and bristling with importance. He was accompanied by a once beautiful woman, with skin of Byzantine gold, which together with the perfect cut of her clothes, and the understated jewelry screamed out spoilt, rich and 'don't even think about messing with me,' thus proclaiming her own aura of consequence.

The airport authorities have a sixth sense about this. In no time our two VIPs were whisked away into the land of a better class of person.

You know what these charter flights were like, rugby scrums with suntan lotion.

"Excuse me."

"Do you mind!"

"I'm sorry!" revolving round the cabin; everybody tired, tetchy and eager to get home, with a few determined spirits, keeping the party going singing, "Viva Espana." There was one seat left. By the window. And who was blocking the way, but the important twosome spotted earlier. No wonder they were grumpy. No first class.

"Is the seat taken?"

"No!" But the tone was Leonidas with the Persians at Thermopylae.

I hesitated. The stewardess pushed me into the seat, ramming my case into the overhead bin, in the process scratching two bags fragrant with saddle soap.

Conversation was going to be tricky. "Did you enjoy your holiday?" I said to break the ice. They stared ahead, simmering. At what, the existence of lesser mortals like myself, the fact that I had scooped the window seat? I gave up.

Ten minutes into the flight, I sensed a crisis looming. All that coffee taken that morning for hangover aversion wanted to go somewhere. Desperately, I tried making my bladder submit, locking my knees against the shoulders of the person in front. Any tighter and I might strangle him. The meal came, making matters worse.

"Excuse me. I have to go." No sign of receiving any message beyond tightening of jaws. "I really *have* to go!" They both stared at me, Cerberus and his missus, the Gatekeepers of Hell.

"You could at least wait till the meal is over."

A lapse of two minutes, then, "Please!"

"You could have waited till they cleared away the trays."

"If I don't go…" I had no need to finish the sentence. The quondam beauty maneuvered her right knee fractionally towards me. "Go!" She commanded. I stood up, and by dint of pushing and grunting managed to get both my legs past her right knee, but her left leg was locked, jammed against the in-flight magazine pocket. I pushed and shoved. My situation was desperate. I tried to dream up the Sahara, but all I saw was rain pouring into Loch Lomond. If I didn't get out pronto there would be a mischief. My pushing was driving my lady's beautiful aquamarine chiffon skirt with its interesting Salvador Dali motif waist-wards. In my current position it would take a very smart brief to get me off a rape charge. She kicked. I slipped. Automatically my hand went out to break my fall. It landed on her starboard bosom. My remark to lighten the load, "I feel a right tit, now," didn't go down too well. John Bull looked as if he were going to punch me. Luckily, I had gone to a school, which specialized in athletics, and executed a neat Western Roll that saw me over a set and a half of legs to dive smoothly into the gangway. Did I mention the excellent *coq du vin* now upended in her shimmering lap? Did I mention the shrieks accompanying displacement not drowned out by those passengers, still hanging onto the holiday spirit, giving me a lusty cheer?

Ah! How sweet was the Relief of Mafeking!

Then.

Attracted by the commotion a hefty task force was gathered round my seat. The stewardess was trying to console the stricken woman.

"My best Christian La Croix totally ruined! And we're supposed to be going to the bishop's garden party this afternoon!" She wailed. The head cabin steward was taking notes. The apoplectic man was crying out, "It's the airline's fault, allowing drunks to board the plane." Evidently the row was of sufficient seriousness to take the flight captain away from the controls. For there he was patting the angry man on the back. He turned to me, his expression clearly saying, "And what the fuck are you going to do about this?"

"I'll sue the bloody airlines, I will!"

Then she saw me. Any classical scholar wanting to know what the Furies were really like, just call this number. "Do you have any idea how much this dress cost, you little turd? You'll pay! You'll pay!" Harmonizing splendidly with this in his rich basso profundo was the red-faced man, snarling like a big cat before breakfast. "Yes, you'll pay. You sniveling jock strap of an excuse for a human being!"

Rather than wait to being savaged, I immediately offered to pay for the dry cleaning. "It's bloody well ruined." She spat out. To add to my embarrassment the passengers were getting their money's worth. If I was get off the plane without being murdered or handcuffed, I had to do something serious so I offered to buy a new dress. Anything to get out of this jam, I waved a credit card about. This abated their ferocity somewhat. No. But a cheque would do. They demanded my name and address. I gave it. I don't know if Roger Rabbit c/o The Bunny Warren, East Neuk, Fife, ever got the bill. All I cared about was getting off that plane quickly.

A week later, I was sitting in Elena's 'Withdrawing' room, which had similar proportions and décor to a ballroom in a cruise liner. In the face of stiff competition, she was the most snobbish by far of my wife's chums. Ignored and bored as usual, I was idly flicking through the latest installment of Good Housekeeping. I stopped, I gasped, I pointed. Elena paused regally in mid anecdote; her purchase of a new pair of shoes was too exciting to brook any interruption.

"It's *them!*" And there they were in a full double page spread, my old dining chum complete with attendant wife, seated in baronial splendor in their charming mansion in the Yorkshire Wolds, known locally as Welcome Hall, but now emerging from their incognito as the Marquis and Lady Kettlewell. With not the slightest trace of aristocratic condescension they were demonstrating for the sake of the humble readers how to achieve connubial bliss by having the good taste to live amidst opulent surroundings. I was pleased to note that Lady Kettlewell was once again faultlessly, not to say spotlessly attired.

"Do you know them?" asked Elena, her voice not making up its mind between envy and heavy sarcasm.

"Know them? Why we dined together, and they were so taken by me they begged me for my address so we could keep in touch. Entirely their idea."

For just a moment Elena looked totally defeated, but recovered neatly, "You'll never guess how much I paid for these *Jimmy Choos?*" But from then on she couldn't have been nicer if I had taken tea with the Queen.

Las Vegas

"Blackjack or craps, your game?" My fellow passenger with the features of a freeze dried Genghis Khan went on. "I play the slots." Without much luck, I thought judging by the frayed cuffs and lustreless eyes. But then three days on a Greyhound bus can do that to you.

"He's goin' to climb the casino tower." This was the obligatory smartass sitting behind me whose knees had been making indentations on my shoulder blades for three days, and who had spent the trip making the moves on the pretty Chicana girl squashed up against the window. None of the itinerant wierdos on the bus believed I was going to Las Vegas to climb mountains. Not the disillusioned Mormon missionary, wearing the ordained underwear that showed up Eve's nakedness. No, I never did find out. She had gone to Britain to redeem our souls from paganism, but instead found British men and socialized medicine wonderful. The trip was the high spot of her life, she said.

Not the Los Angelino boy from the 'Hood, whose chat line was, "Me and the brothers stole your car in LA other day." "How many brothers do you have?" I asked mock naively, to be rewarded by a chorus of knee slapping chortles from the lads in the back. See we were one big happy family till he got hauled off the bus and arrested in Denver for possession. "It's only cause I'm black." He cried out from under a scrum of five guardians of the law. It was my introduction to the heavy handedness of the American police, maybe; sometimes it pays not to jump to conclusions. All in all it was an educational ride. And just like in school, one of the passengers was expelled for smoking in the bog. A harsh penalty as he was dumped in the bleak wastelands of Kansas, but as the driver said, "If you're gonna break the rules, check your shoe leather as that's your alternative mode of transportation."

Although I was sustained in this uncomfortable journey by keeping in mind my destination, I had difficulty visualizing the sandstone cliffs described by Gary save as Harrison's rocks swathed in neon lit ads. The only outdoors shots of Vegas I had seen were of Bond out for an early morning car chase. It was difficult to get beyond his dapper profile, but if you could manage it there was a blue sky overhanging a dusty plain broken by the odd clump of cactus.

Meeting my new American comrades the talk was of 5.12s and other mathematical abstractions. As my eyes glazed over I couldn't help thinking climbers are the same the world over, eager to bore them in the aisles at a moment's notice. We camped in the desert. It was late November, a month I associate with damp days tramping over Bleaklow's muddy plateau, but here the sun shone amiably over a cheerful russet landscape A roadrunner skittered across our path disappearing in a puff of dust as if life was copying the cartoon. Further down the track, a herd of wild burros was munching with relish what were evidently gourmet cactus spines. How could anyone prefer the tawdry town with its dial a hooker service to this other Eden?

And all at once this far away place was familiar. The cacti, sagebrush and tumbleweed dancing across the sand with the hazy hint of hills in the background stirred my memory back to Saturday mornings in The

Roxy watching Hopalong Cassidy riding across the prairie shooting at the baddies conveniently clad in dark hats and dark mustaches. These Red Rock canyons may have been the ideal klettergarten, but I could only see it as the perfect place for an Apache ambush. For me the magic of the setting was its constant evocation of those innocent days.

The frost crackled on the tent opening the door next morning. During the night the temperature dropped with the speed of a finger snap; a signal for the coyotes to set up their howling chorus not yards away from the tents. Shouldn't I have checked my trainers for scorpions? That thought only occurred to me after I lurched onto the cold sand of the arroyo. Used to the aquiline symmetry of Alpine peaks whose coarse rocky bits were softened by snowy, silken sheets, these great rusty mastodons of crags out of a science fiction comic staggered my preconceptions with their gigantic leggo bricks arranged in fantastic pyramids, smote and smelted by some Promethean behemoth.

"How big is that?" asked Tim pointing to a slab winking in the sunlight like a freshly baked biscuit. "200' at most." I said. "It's over a thousand feet high!" Sure, I thought, till later I found he had underestimated. The clarity of the desert air made it seem near and miniscule. We drove out in a wide loop skirting the desert to Willow Springs, a ravine with a passing resemblance to a miniature Llanberis. Like on any Sunday back home, people were gossiping between climbs, enjoying watching the rise and fall of the inept, while admiring the designer teams flipping their way through the guide book climbs with contemptuous ease, finishing with heart stopping free 150' rappels off the polished stems of vegetables that you hoped were sturdy enough to see them through the weekend, bearing in mind the maxim that traveling hopefully is better than arriving too suddenly. Completing the nostalgic moment was a van load of yobboes playing rock music that bounced from wall to wall of the canyon at maximum decibels, exercising their constitutional right to annoy everyone else. Only the funny labels on the beer cans chucked out of their van and baseball hats back to front bespoke a foreign place.

An unusual feature of the climbing here was the ancient petroglyphs carved on the red rocks in prehistoric times. Grunting up the layback crack of our first climb, I scrupulously avoided treading on the inflated dicks etched on the wall just south of my toe. Their owners looked like they were enjoying themselves, these frozen in time monuments, the only remnants of the Paiute tribe. They must have been formidable climbers to carve these magnificent dongers so high up the wall without modern gear.

Three days later we walked into the splendid Pine Creek Canyon to tackle The Cat in the Hat, a superb climb undersold by its funky title. Mescalito, the mountain whose offspring it was, was a sandstone Hershey's Kiss, framed by a canyon whose walls, rocks and torrents had been writhed, twisted and ripped apart by Brobdingnagian forces erupting from the innards of the earth, as if a mad Gothic painter had been let loose to feast his imagination on a post apocalyptic vision of the inferno. Every rope length was elegant, intrinsically interesting in harmony with its neighbors and more to the point only mildly severe in standard. The first pitch a long sinuous crack raddled with huecos, cupboard size holes in the rock, uncurled like a whiplash at the top, to be followed by an amiable layback, and then a Chinese puzzle of a crux wall, harder by far than the rest of the climb, complete with a bowel collapsing vista of the arroyo bed far below. Gratifyingly the rope was tight as a piano wire, and after a few sweaty moves all such concern was academic. The final four pitches, a soaring slab that went on and on till it peaked out onto a headwall were the *ne plus ultra* of this superb climb. Gary and I toasted ourselves in the agreeable November sunshine, wondering about the petroglyph carved high on the climb, which was of a scarab, a dung beetle, a favorite icon of the Ancient Egyptians. What was it doing so high up? Had the

Paiute levitated to this point? But then what was it doing in the Western Hemisphere? Was it evidence of a pre Colombian crossing of the Pond by a restlessly wandering Pharaoh? We never did find the answer.

Then we made our mistake. Instead of calling it quits on our nice little ledge, and abseiling back down reasonably early, we decided *'to go for the top.'* The guidebook had optimistically telescoped the grade three trudges so that three pitches on the printed page turned out to be six on the stone. In this case after scrambling up decaying vegetable matter we found we had only surmounted a shoulder, and were still only on the caramel cream section of the candy, the raspberry topping still out of reach. Calling upon a dishonorable tradition dating back to the 'first ascent' of Denali, Gary took a discretely angled "summit" snap and we retreated.

The sun slid down behind the canyon rim as we began the rappels. By the time we hit the last rappel there was only a glimmer of light left. I slid gingerly down into the night. About 50' below my head torch picked out the flimsy bramble bush hung with tat that should have been our last point of departure. Way, way below, I could see the rope fizzling out into darkness like a fishing line in murky water. When I did my first bounce onto terra firma I had five feet of rope left. A fall into a cactus bush completed my adventure. Gary could hardly pull me out for laughing. Maybe I am a poor sport, but I couldn't see the funny side; after all a pepper-potted bottom is a series of sore points.

Outcropping the next day, we met the man from Idaho whose hobby was buffeting. Las Vegas, working on the mousetrap principle with its collation of cheap eateries, was buffet man's heaven. He only climbed, he said in a drawl so deep you could grow potatoes in it, to put an edge on his appetite. He must have been pretty hungry for he was lolloping up the cliff at approximately ten feet per word. We took his advice and dined medievally at the Excalibur, a recreation of Camelot complete with polystyrene Gothic turrets. Our servitors were Hispanic jesters and wenches accoutered in a medley of fashions plucked indiscriminately from across the centuries. Today was Thanksgiving, a holiday I was to love and revere, but at this stage impressed me as an excuse for an all American guzzle fest, a freedom to be a fatty, an unwritten clause in the Bill of Rights. Crammed with turkey and accessories, I wandered the slot machine rows each occupied by a fat person armed with a McDonald cup filled with quarters. I put a quarter in a vacant machine, lost it, but I could say to the folks back in Blighty that I had gambled in Vegas. How often do we do things to impress our indifferent friends?

Surprisingly, I liked Vegas. Its sleazy wedding chapels, its blatantly cheerful money grubbing, its no one is fooled fakery attained a level of ebullient vulgarity that Blackpool could only dream about. Early next morning we left the modern Babylon, crossing the desert by following a gap in the line of cacti. Slowly the horizon rim turned into the palest of blues, then the sun hit the Solar Slab igniting it in a cold fire. Today's climb was the severe climber's dream line. The first six pitches took us up a gully via ribs of vertical granite garnished with plate like jugs and incuts giving access to the cactus groves that were our belay stances. On the slab the sun hit us with surprising venom, searing the backs of our necks and knees. Even four liters of water was not enough to prevent us feeling like chickens on a broiler.

Gary led off up a stunning knight's move pitch that from the stance seemed overhanging but on encounter turned out to be an amenably corrugated slab. When I reached the ledge the sun was dropping over Gary's shoulder, telling us not to linger any longer. I went at the next pitch, a gigantic whalebone lying against the slab. Two super pitches tracked their way over the slab finishing up an overhanging bulge, which turned out to be another *trompe d'oeil* furnished with solid jughandles. Standing on the skimpy stance looking over the magnificent vista of mountains and desert reminded me of similar moments in the Alps, even though the wild west scenery couldn't have been more different. I kept having to remind myself that this was November the time for making lugubrious dank treks across the Peak, not gadding about on sun blanched rock. Feeling confident I led up a long crack system. I shook a bit but as my limbs kept hitting holds I maintained upward momentum. Another similar pitch followed, and then the last rampart; a neat little corner crack reminiscent of a Lake District Severe, here in God's Own Country. That should have been it but the route refused to stop. Slabs pretty in pink, but now an ominous reminder of how low the sun was, ground tediously up for another three long pitches.

At last we were done. We coiled our ropes by an opal green pool scooped out of a potsherd red bowl. Far below we could see dusk scudding across the desert, and in a pool of darkness that was Las Vegas the lights came out twinkling like fireflies. Somewhere down there Dean Martin was sipping his first martini.

Three times we tried to find a way down but each ended in a *cul de sac*. Fourth time lucky; we found the signpost, a tangle of slings tied to a cactus root. Three drops later we found ourselves looking over a cliff as high as a skyscraper. I turned to Gary. The expression on his face told me we were in deep trouble. A dangerous bit of soloing only led us into another *cul de sac*. We moved back up and in the next gully in that last dim daylight we could just discern a rappel point.

Throwing the rope down we heard a hearty slap telling us it had hit bottom. I couldn't say my heart was in my mouth, when I roped down as my flashlight was already there. Without a head torch it did the business, but I lost the taste for plastic long before I reached the ground.

We abseiled over inky voids, through gauntlets of spiky cacti, every so often being impaled by an unusually malignant plant. Our worst fear was

153

our rope not reaching bottom, but we had to trust to luck. After fifteen such leaps we saw level ground ahead.

"Assholes!" said Gary. I came out with something more fundamentally Anglo-Saxon. We were on a flat slab still high above the valley floor. We lay down both knackered. Out on the rim of the slab the pale blue ribbon that marked the horizon was engulfed by the night. A solitary cactus of the finger and thumb variety was pointing upwards into the black vault of the heavens, brilliantly emblazoned by a thousand stars. Two shooting stars leapt out of nowhere, then perished without trace.

"Hey, Gav, over here!" While I was taking in the scenery, Gary had been busy. I followed the tilt of the slab and found him rigging up the next set of abseils. Once again we were on the long haul of threading up and sliding down the ropes, when Gary began laughing. He recognized the medley of slings. Somewhere we had lost the descent and were following the line of the route. Quite abruptly there were no more abseils. Sheer luck had placed us back from where we started. We coiled the rope and took the *fires* from our burning feet.

Naturally we lost our way in the arroyo, but later much later found ourselves in a motel room. Outside you could see the fake marble halls of Caesar's Palace. Someone had made a serious effort to put up accurate replicas of Roman statues. There was Marcus Aurelius, the philosopher emperor, flanked by Julius Caesar and Augustus, giving his blessing to one of the least philosophical enterprises in Western Civilization.

But it was time to go. Every one was catching planes. There was one comrade left, who said, "It is quite in order to take a shower." He said it several times so I knew we had returned to civilization. I breakfasted in a casino, where they asked me to keep my shoes on. The family man at the next table wore a T-shirt with the legend, "If you don't like my attitude, dial 1-800-eat shit." I wondered what Marcus Aurelius would say to that. On the bus home I sat beside an Apache Indian who made a scissor sign and said," White Man he talk with fork tongue." Honestly, but I wasn't to take it personally.

The Sandwich Bag

At this stage, I really ought to introduce myself. Let's just call me Jake. Everyone else does. What my real name is, well let's just say no names, no pack drill, and leave it at that. If you met me outside my milieu, you would think, 'singularly unpleasant person' and steer a wide berth. Why? I've got what they call a speech impediment, which puts some off, I guess, but it's more my eyes make people nervous. You see they meet at a point well short of infinity, making me look the kind of guy as would steal the sugar out of Granny's tea, and as you tend to live up to the way people treat you… enough said. You wouldn't call me a thief. Some do, but it's more like picking up stuff people leave around, that sort of level. You might call it tidying up. And I stare. Don't ask me why; it's something I can't help. Once a woman just out of the blue, punched me for seemingly no reason, but on a guess I would say it was that stare. Obviously I don't have many friends, zilch in the female sector. I had a girl friend once, a Play-boy Centerfold, and then I woke up. Most of my pursuits are solitary. Being alone, I read a lot. Suppose that helps my lacking education. That's all I've got.

I met her in the local rock gym, my turf. I would say my habitat, but bearing in mind all the things you must have heard about me by now, you might think I were a talking chimp. One thing I do really well is climb.

You name it rock, plastic stuck on concrete, garden walls, trees, I'm your man. On my home ground people overlook my drawbacks, because I am a star, well not so much of a star, more of an asteroid. Folk don't exactly flock to my mat to tie on to my rope, but some come for instruction when nothing else is available. This modest species of parliamentary privilege goes as far as the gym door not a step further where social intercourse continues its foreordained pattern.

That day she came for a lesson she just about threw the whole place into turmoil, she was so beautiful, far too beautiful for this place, hardly in the same galaxy. For me she was too unreal, like these models in Vogue who are too airily, haughtily gorgeous you can't get a hand job off them. She marched right up to me as if she were on a mission from Mars. I was the only one who would do for instruction.

"My name's Wendy. No I don't wear pigtails. Remember that and we could be friends." Because she was so eerily inappropriately divinely beautiful, I felt no need to seize up. Sensibly I didn't say much, but let my climbing do the talking, drifting up the wall like wood-smoke. I sensed appreciation for my buffed biceps and glossy calves rippling under the garish strip lighting.

For such an elegant swan she climbed brutally, all staccato lunges, and grabs, but as fearless as you can be in the unimaginative surrounds of a rock gym. If she persisted she might become good. When stripped for action she was surprisingly muscular, more the Cumean Sybil than a fragile flower of femininity, but when dressed she was as feminine as Grace Kelly. She could be moody, changeable, like they say about the weather in Ohio. If you don't like it wait five minutes, bright sunny vistas, then the boom of thunder, and a torrent of weeping skies. Dark forbidding clouds would lower upon her brow whenever the seriously cool guys tried hitting on her. The unexpected bursts of sunshine always came in my direction. Don't ask me why.

It was her second visit that saw the beginning of all my hopes and trials. She stepped up to the wall, ready for me to give her a safety once over. Checking her harness tripped a teeny erotic ripple, too small to be detected by any body part, but it caught me off balance. The other guys were forever bragging about getting tits in their faces, and climbing with an extra limb. I never got a jolt on the job. No tit was pushed in my face. Any I stared at, turned and faced the other way.

She lunged at the holds with tremendous drive. Tackling overhangs she kept at it till her fingers turned to butter and she peeled off totally beat. Teaching in a rock gym is dull and predictable. All these instructors wearing that careless aura of cool and arrogance haven't caught up with the fact that their chosen avocation is as exciting as manning the check-out at Kroger's, less if you ask me. The occasional flash in the otherwise flat pan sparked off by getting hot under the chalk-bag when fixing chicks harnesses, or far more infrequently spotting genius in the making. The combination of both is a rare treat making you think for a while that you are not such a sad person.

For some odd reason she took to me, phoning me all hours with any excuse to prattle. Perhaps she collected oddities, or reveled in the company of misfits, otherwise why bother with me. Anything approximating a joke from me, and she would near burst her butt laughing. When she invited herself out for a drink with me after climbing, I wasn't thrown into a tizzy, for at this stage I couldn't believe she had any interest in me. So no *pavor muliebris*, a Freudian term, I just made up, for those struck dumb whenever any female comes visiting. So when she said, "How about we go to the Rope and Anchor? I'll buy the pints and you can put me right on where to place my feet."

"You buying? You kidding?"

"Right let's off then!"

I never asked her how come I was chosen, when the gym was heaving with muscle, guys with third day stubble, so never found out. Nor did I discover where she came from. Later when we became friendly enough to chat freely, the area devoted to antecedents was invariably glossed over cursorily. So efficient was the erasure it wasn't till I put my thinking cap for the purpose of these recollections that I noticed it. It wasn't a long road for me given my uncomely appearance, and prior lack of attention from the fair sex. Just a little twitch on the thread, the sudden flash of a smile in my direction and I was the mouse looking at the cheese, wondering what that great big spring was for. Thus Caliban, thus Quasimodo.

How does the story go from here? It's fairly obvious. Quasimodo only needed Esmeralda to be nice for him to tumble. Wendy was nice to me, very touchy feely. When she touched my arm, even lightly, an electric shock went straight to my cock. A woman touching my flesh voluntarily! Is it any wonder I was done for? For me she was a beautiful woman in all weathers, but from others I heard mutters, "That's some mean bitch of a bitch." But then they were just jealous.

"Never let on that you fancy a bird, because once you do you've lost the war." Which translated goes, let a chick know you have the hots for her, and you're screwed. This little nugget of wisdom came from my English buddy, Terry. We were in The Bag of Nails expiating on Man's eternal problem, Eve, the Bite on the Apple, and how to get a pint of decent warm beer minus froth. Terry was my only real buddy. He picked me out deliberately because he saw in me a fellow odd duck, who could float in his idiosyncratic pond. Since he was virtually the only person I spoke to, and I read a lot, my language comes out as a costive farrago of Mancunian slang lumped in with strained renderings of nineteenth century Jamesian diction. Ouch! We were supping this gaseous pint of faux Boddingtons. "Nowt like they make it in Manchester." With this verdict out of the way, we moved onto a serious discussion about Wendy. When I explained her to him, instead of saying, "Lucky sod," he went, "Watch thy step, sunshine."

"How come?"

"A woman like that doesn't know her mind. She's playing all the cards in the deck, and playing's the word, once she's discarded you, she'll bring you down, as sure as," He reached out for some handy metaphor, "Wendy wears pigtails." That had me beat- her hair had more changes than the weather, but of pigtails nada- till I realized he was talking of Wendy, the presiding goddess of Columbus' burger empire.

....

It was about then that Taylor MacKinzie entered the lists of the Dramatis Personae. The tall languid Texan sauntered into the gym. Announcing himself as from the Lone Star State, with his "Howdy, Y'all," a salutation that took a while to render, for each syllable was stretched to breaking point; the other pointer being the Stetson wedged on an escarpment of his coiffure, headgear not often seen in Columbus, Ohio. This friendly greeting was met with the blank stares accorded to outsiders. Altogether too GQ probably missed his way in the mall. "Suffrin' sarsaparilla! No-one tawkin' here?" No one talked. The silence was broken by a squeal from Wendy, just as I was trying on a new belaying technique demanding close attention and closer bodily contact. As she was tied onto me, the rope pulled her down like a leash on an overexcited dog. I remembered what others had called her.

In minutes Taylor had thrown out a web of charisma. Wendy was netted right away, bobbing up and down like a sixteen year old. I too was sucked in by his magnetism, for he possessed the knack, not uncommon amongst successful people when introduced to strangers, of making them believe he had been waiting his whole life to make their acquaintance. Such an intense infusion of bonhomie targeted so precisely leaves the recipient decidedly gingered up.

Wendy was whisked away from me easily. She had never been mine, but I fooled myself I was closing in steadily, having taken her on several exclusive trips to Seneca. In a moment he had seized the ground I had so laboriously worked over, but I was still glowing from his handshake, thinking how lucky I was to be in his company, and of course what right had I to claim Wendy, who was totally out of my class. My cock eyed gawp must have frightened her, like it did the rest. Later, when Taylor's magic had faded, I smarted.

With impressive speed off the mark, Taylor was signed on as the designated boyfriend. At least she was decent enough to keep me in the holding pen to lean on in a lean time, till the Lone Ranger came up with the goods, under that dreaded rubric, "A friend." I was told his company was grooming him on the fast track for the top. No surprise there. Wendy was still interested in climbing, especially absolutely adoring Seneca, but it was only her feet and hands that were on the rock, her heart and head were in a more fantastical place. I bit my nails wondering when or if he had yet swept her out of her panties, while speculating on what non-commercial impulse had driven MacKinzie into the gym, when clearly the place, with its dirt and its losers disgusted him. Apparently his firm smiled on the character building aspects of rock-climbing, and so he was here to pad out his resume. The company, which specialized in baking humongous burgers, insisted their top executives be slim and lithe as athletes- more decorative in the company's PR blurbs- while doing their bit towards creating a race of sumo wrestlers. Climbing, which did not involve excessive bruising or the booze intake concomitant with American football, seemed just the ticket with of course the unanticipated plus for

Taylor of being the shortest route into Wendy's undies. There was one glimmer of relief in this picture, in that behind a desk Taylor may have been soared like an eagle, but on the wall a turkey was the only thing on a wing he resembled, while at the other end of the gym Wendy was pretty good, as well as being pretty. He was so embarrassing I squirmed. Whenever he put hand on hold, the smart asses would crowd round pretending to spot him, and then when he fell let him drop. What a riot! Who said climbers weren't prepubescent misfits? Naturally that got him down. If people tend to like the things they are good at, the opposite is also true, so he began the slow drift away from the gym towards a more amenable habitat. Wendy was pulled both ways. She had taken to climbing majorly, still calling me at all hours to drag me off to our forbidden Eden, Springfield Gorge, but I could sense something amiss.

But how could I compete with Taylor plucking her up by chopper and dropping her into the governor's box at Buckeye Field? How tempting was a rain swept weekend nestling in a tent at Seneca compared to a masked ball in Venice? In her hotel suite nestling on her pillow as a substitute for a chocolate treat was a ring with a stone bigger than a walnut whirl. She told me this as we summited the slender razor back of Seneca's South Peak on a gorgeous summer evening. For just a moment the panorama was blotted out by a black cloud of hatred. "What would you have done?" She looked at me imploringly, like there had been a titanic struggle for the possession of her soul, and that she had been an unwilling Eurydice towed away from a tuneless Orpheus.

She was dying to show me the ring, tucked safely in her chalk bag. Of course I refused to look at it. Then when she had taken to the bushes to visit the 'bathroom,' I peeped in and saw she was telling no lie. Luckily I rejected the temptation to chuck it after her, but I felt sick and sulked while she was radiant, wittering on about the beauties of nature when really she was thinking of the beauties of the House of Seven Bathrooms, monogrammed bath towels and popcorn bowls by Hermes, overlooking Muirfield golf course, for all of which the ring was a mere promissory note.

Is it snide of me hinting that the ring was a way over the top peace offering after a lover's tiff had led to a temporary rift? Taylor had indulged himself in this intermission by taking off with his secretary, a lady whose understanding of the pressures he was going through was rewarded by this mini-break promotion.

I had no idea what was going on, when she came to the gym, her shoulders all slumped, dragging her feet, and climbing like an un-milked cow. After sufficient groans and moans had heralded a baleful announcement, I said, "Would you like to have a serious conversation about this, or shall we take as our topic something droll, frivolous or mad-cap?" She stared at me in disbelief and then said, "Fuck off and listen asshole." I listened. I listened some more when I bought her too much to drink at The Shepherdess and her Crook -some Disneylander's idea of an English pub- and some more when I took her home and she spewed up over my lap, after accusing me of deliberately getting her drunk.

"Is this your big idea; tie one on me to get my pussy juicy?" She was smiling when she said it, so I wasn't too discouraged.

"Who me?" She needed a little comforting, so I took her in my arms and gave her a big slushy kiss. She didn't call out the sheriff so after a polite interval for getting her used to the idea, my hands started romping over hill and dale. A lot of heavy breathing let me think tonight's the night. "Get Lucky!" The motto on my baseball cap spoke to me forcibly. Even though the reference was to a brand of cigarettes, the omens were right on. My hands slid southwards. The heavy breathing came to a sudden stop, and a decidedly unimpassioned voice said, "What do you think you're up to?"

Pushing me back into the bowl of cat-litter handily placed for dishing upstarts.

"Don't you ever, ever come near me ever again!" Well that was that with knobs on, so I went home as depressed and miserable as I had been elated earlier.

Two days later the phone rang. "Guess what?"

"What?"

"Taylor has just handed me the most gorgeous ring you ever did see." I forbore to ask her about Ms Factotum at the office and presumed she had been bought off with promotion out of state. I did say to her, "I thought I was never to speak to you ever again for, like, eternity?" "Oh that. Silly me! And silly you. Of course, we are still friends, but I absolutely forbid any bodily contact."

"Hadn't he given you a ring already?"

"Oh that! Compared to this that one came out of a corn flake packet."

And she went on to describe it, but I held the phone away and went on knawing at my double cheeseburger. "And of course you are to be our best man." That got my ear to the phone. I managed to blurt out, though I don't know how, "Congratulations to you both." Before collapsing in a heap crying.

Oddly enough MacKinzie had taken a real liking to me, as opposed to the false *bonhomie* of his Hail, fellow, well-met routine. Why? Some people like having a pet monkey beside them for comparison's sake. I was Sancho Panza to his questing knight, Wendy being Dulcinea, the windmills tilted at … There your guess is as good as mine. Because of my long standing friendship of five months with bride and groom the fabulous ring was entrusted to my safe keeping, an honor as enticing as a face rub from a hedgehog. A more intense version of the treatment came later that week when Wendy came bouncing into the gym with an assignment, "Jake, you're gonna take me to Seneca."

"Why?"

"I need to say farewell to the mountain I love. MacKinzie's told me to say *Arrivederci* to climbing, and a big *Ciao* to serving cocktails to fat office cats. I've been nominated butt-kisser to the throne." She paused to see how I would take this news, and smiled. "Like giving him a shoulder on his climb up the corporate ladder."

"Like being home help Sherpa."

"You sound bitter. Please don't. There's no need." What could I say to that? The weeks before the wedding had been hell for me. Everyone was talking nothing but wedding plans, and all I wanted to do was get out of town. "Sure why not. It will also be our last time together. No way will I fit into the court of Taylor MacKinzie." It was a plea, it was a whine, begging for reassurance, but Wendy said nothing. Her brow furrowed for a flickering second, then she recovered with an agility that would stand her in good stead in those arduous evenings ahead, all night on her feet in Jimmy Choos, nibbling at her rumaki, nursing that glass of 97 Chateau Mouton Rothschild, wondering why she still preferred a Sam Adams; all the while boning up on her Ladies-Who-Lunch Patter for Dummies in preparation for audience with the CEO's wife, or life partner as she now preferred to be called, whose *memento mori* features would give Hieronymus Bosch a sleepless night. She leapt up, hugged me and smacked a sisterly snog on my cheek. This was the nearest I had ever got to permissible bodily contact.

"Awesome! I can't wait." She screamed, dancing like a dainty dervish at my side.

We climbed Ecstasy in glorious conditions, surrounded by autumn leaves quivering gently in ruby red splendor. Both of us were climbing well. Afterwards we sat in the sunny bower at the top of the climb coiling the ropes, and soaking in the immense satisfaction of a climb well done. For some reason she decided to torment me with the saga of The Wedding Dress, the trouble with the pearl beading; her mum having to seal her into her crinoline. For any other female personage I would have screamed, but being alone with her on this sublime mountain I was in that state of delirium I could have listened to her raining down curses upon my head, and all my forebears and progeny too, and still been enchanted. After a lunch break we sauntered up to the foot of the Green Wall, possibly the most elegant climb on the mountain.

I started up. Wendy glided up after me, the gear chinking musically on her belt as she smoothly extracted Friends, Rocks and Stoppers placed by me. As always she looked good in her powder blue outfit, she even managed to find a matching chalk bag. This lady knew how to accessorize. In no time we were coiling ropes on the peak. The top of Seneca Rocks consists of a large angular boulder perched precariously on top of a narrow fin of rock above a vertical four hundred foot drop on both sides. A meteorite might have impaled itself on the razor keen ridge. We sat by the old ammunition box holding the climbing log, gazing out to space, as lazy as the hawk riding thermals, circling the mountain. He was an old friend from a beloved place. In the background the purple ridges of the Appalachians shimmered in a blue haze.

"Jake, I think I am falling in love again." I stirred from my slumber hopefully. "With this place. Oh Jake! I have never felt so much about somewhere as I do here." "Yea, sure." I replied unable to match her mood. "This is where I belong, where I will always want to be." She pointed in the general direction of the sultry valley intoning. "Let my ashes be strewn from this mountain peak in West Virginia." Women, I thought. Even when they think they are joking they're not." But I loved her nonsense, and found myself, humming, 'Almost Heaven, West Virginia.' And it was. It was.

Then up pops MacKinzie, puffing and shaking like an old dog, having been hauled up Old Lady's Route by a guide, hired at short notice. Why he insisted on driving alone to meet us was a mystery, since however chummy he might appear on the surface, at heart, like every one else he considered me a joke; nor was he the jealous type with last minute vapors about me being a threat. Like any rich dude, MacKinzie was possessive of his new property.

With him there everything was spoilt. Now ugly black clouds began building up round the mountain.

Just then a sudden draught of air whipped up a rain shower. "C'mon we need to go before the rock gets slick." I handed her the rope. She shook her head. "No, don't need it."

"I'll take care of her now, Jake. Your time is up." If it was a joke, it didn't come out like one. Wendy added softly, "Thanks, Jake, I'll be OK with Taylor from here. We'll see you back at the campsite." While this was going on MacKinzie was grinning at me licking his lips, like he was signaling, 'This you never will taste.' I wanted to smash his stupid shitty chops. I didn't, which was wise as he was unroped, and would have gone over, and that would have been murder.

The guide shrugged. He was like, do I get paid for putting up with this crap? Well the lovebirds were both grown up, and I didn't have the responsibilities the guide had abdicated. Where we were is the narrowest piece of rock with clear drops of hundreds of feet on either side. I scrambled down tensely, as I always did when unroped to the platform below. By this time the rock had got a good spattering. She followed sauntering airily down the soapy slippery summit slab, hands in pockets looking at me superciliously. I held out my hand, but she shook her head laughing, "No touch," before jumping lightly down onto the platform. She laughed again, with Taylor standing behind her, and it hit me as clear as daylight who they were laughing at.

The rain began pishing down seriously. "You don't need me to baby you down from here. You both know how to fix up a rappel. I'm going down before I get pissed wet through." I turned my back on them and swung down the first rappel. I knew I shouldn't but I couldn't resist, "Gives you a chance to taste her again." I didn't need to look; his anger was burning into my back. I'm glad she didn't hear that. Wendy looked at me with a bland smile, wondering what was going on between her two boys.

And that was the last memory I had of her. At the inquest Taylor laid the guilt on me fair and square. "He left us. Wendy was scared, and slipped on the wet rock. I tried to hold her, but couldn't manage to keep her. She fell. She fell near four hundred feet!" He had to be taken out of the courtroom he was weeping so much. A witness on a neighboring climb told a different story. "It didn't look like that to me. He was the one that was frightened. He was fixing up his rappel, and had actually clipped in when he slipped on the wet rock. He panicked, grabbed the girl, who was unroped, and pulled her off. The guy was tied into rappel gear, so he was safe all the time.

"How far away were you when the events you described took place?"

"I was on a neighboring climb, West Pole about fifty feet away."

"Was there anything to block your view, a tree for instance? And wouldn't you be too engrossed in your own climb to notice what was going 50 feet away?" A good attorney can sure as heck wipe away sin and take with it a hefty chunk of your pocket book. My pocket was spared but I was rapped pretty hard on the knuckles for leaving a pair of novices to their own devices by the justice.

A week later, what would have been the wedding day dawned clear and achingly beautiful. Reconciled by grief, MacKinzie and I were back at Seneca. From the top of the South Peak a sad cluster of friends emptied polybags full of Wendy's ashes, which immediately were caught and tumbled by the wind swirling in all directions, in a bizarre scene reminiscent of the tornado at the beginning of the *Wizard of Oz.* "She is resting in the place she loved best." MacKinzie started on a speech, but couldn't stop choking and crying. So we watched silently the ashes dispersing on their little clouds, till there was nothing left. Coming down MacKinzie perked up and suggested that tomorrow we should do Wendy's last climb to connect with her. I agreed. Why not? It would cheer us both up.

We were making sandwiches next morning when a knock at the door told us our friends were eager to leave for the hill. Damn, we've run out of poly bags for the sandwiches. I needed just the one for my cheese roll. At the bottom of my sac was an overlooked unemptied bag of cremated ash. Just the job, thinks I, and while Taylor wasn't looking I emptied the last of Wendy down the toilet. Rinsed under the tap a couple of times, the bag looked pretty clean, besides these things were sterile weren't they? My extra thick slab of Red Leicester extra sharp with tomato, a peck of pepper and a slather of mustard, was wrapped round a roll and bagged.

Climbing Wendy's last route was a really bad idea. Watching Taylor furiously wrestling with the short overhang well-stocked with holds where Wendy had waltzed made me want to puke. He was more shaky than usual so I made sure we kept the rope on for the short scramble to the summit

Sitting on top I felt utterly bleak; the memory of last time was so strong. It was with an absent not very gladsome mind that I took my cheese sandwich out of its bag. Hmm! It was more peppery than usual. I put down to the spices we had added. Mind you, the date on the packet told us it had outstayed its welcome. I looked again. The spices were suspiciously grey in appearance. Fuck me! I was eating Wendy's ashes! I remembered being disgusted reading about some French shipwrecked mariners compelled to select the most nutritious of their comrades to provide dinner. Whatever! I was starving. A little bit of dust doth not a cannibal make, so I wiped the roll as clean as I could with hands dirty from climbing. I mustn't have had much of a conscience because I actually chuckled for at that moment I possessed Wendy more thoroughly than I ever had in life. "It's that good?" asked the guileless Taylor. I tickled my mustache with my tongue in a deliberately feeble imitation of his most obnoxious gesture, but now more like a gourmet chef adjudicating *Le Grande Buffet*. The joke was to be mine alone. I warned you I was weird.

"You'll never taste anything so succulent. Why it's as good as an orgasm!"

"Never heard anyone say *that* about a cheese sandwich."

On the rappels down the hill, I was bouncing off the rocks like a US Marine, so effervescently that other teams shouted out,

"What you smokin', man?"

"Where you get it, man?"

But by the time I reached the deck I felt distinctly queasy.

A Day Without a Hug

As if that was not enough the Latin teacher's name was Llanfair- Plin-limmon. The kids, like kids everywhere, too lazy to assimilate difficult novelty, but without the wit to create a fitting nickname, simply called him 'him', pointing to the gloomy cavern, an enlarged storeroom allotted as a classroom for his diminutive groups. Above the door were two signs placed by the incumbent. The first, "Welcome to the Inferno," did not ex- actly fit into the school's positive marketing strategy, and there had been several requests each curter than the last advising him to take it down, or expect 'Consequences,' a value free term when applied to the students, but much more threatening, one might say consequential, when directed at the adult portion of the school community. The other notice scarcely less provocative, stated boldly, 'Hug Free Zone.' In his quiet and under-stated way L.P.-we are not going through all the palaver of trying to spell out again his Celtic moniker- was emblazoning his defiance of what the school stood for, aka the Mission Statement, an effusive rhapsody about an integrated, focused, global, non- judgmental, challenging community, which, when all is said and done, boiled down to a hug and a donut makes all the difference. Though the rest of the school did not know it, this was this Cold Fish's way of having a riot.

"What's this Asshole doin' here?" Taylor Scranton, baseball hat on aft-before-fore in his customary learning posture legs hanging over the shoulders of the student in front, had summed up the thoughts of everyone in the school. In this place, where jollification and kids-speak was the name of the game, and where even the cafeteria ladies greeted each other with a morning hug, LP stuck out like a sore thumb. To these sunshine people, his stern manner and serious purpose brought with it a whiff of the mortuary. There were multiple-choice answers to Taylor's question. Young Ryan, ninth grade, opined that he had swum the Rio Grande to get here, and claimed his hair still reeked of the garlicky stench of Mexico's most famous river. Others were unanimous that he was a mail order husband for a donut dame, who had gone to Lisdoonvarna a week too late to catch a hubby, and had trusted her all in a magazine's cut price offer, but when she saw the goods had fled to Texas. The currently most popular theory was that he was the first and up till now only homosexual war bride brought home by a lonely G.I. The fate of the husband was unknown; dead, divorced, or escaped over the state line, he was now not on the scene.

"He stinks and he's crap." Murph O'Toole, spoke for all in their evaluation of their alien classics master. His enthusiasts were a rare breed, and you could search high and low before finding the few outcasts, book in hand with a tepidly fond word for our L.P. In theory the parents liked the idea of his toffee-nosed voice elevating the tone of their nouveau riche establishment, but his clipped uptight accent grated on them and his precise consonants appeared to be a never-ending reproach to their free and easy wind of the prairie mode of expression. In particular Abe Thomas, one of the school's heavy hitters, complained that when he gave his traditional greeting, "Wat'sup, homies!" L.P. looked at him, "like I'd just farted." Little did they know and this was the irony of it all that his posh sounding speech was that of the South Wales Coalmines. If they did latch on they would probably have asked for their money back, but then who can tell?

No one could see how good, bad or indifferent a Latin teacher he was nor did anyone really care. The kids hated his stern taskmaster approach, and his failure to provide bribes such as candies or vouchers for the dress down days, which filled a goodly proportion of their calendar, seemed to many an independent observer to be a deliberate flouting of recognized practice in educating the offspring of the extremely rich. An occasional muttered, 'not bad' was a hollow substitute for the ecstatic 'Wonderfuls!' heaped on them from the homegrown faculty, who had all majored in child-centered pedagogy. At times his bitter sarcasm was just too much for the children, who would fling themselves weeping into the ample bosoms of their warm-hearted English teacher. She had armchairs and dress up costumes in her room for the kids to do little skits and forget about the dark world lurking down the corridor. "Tell us about the boy, who broke his grandma's heart when he was bad at school, Miz Reims." They chorused. The kids slouched placidly half-listening to the tale, which somehow managed to involve a horrible ogre of a teacher uncannily like our hero bullying a little boy, whose only fault was he never listened or did as he was told. Why? Because the bully master was out to get at the little guy's self esteem.

"But one day his grandma came to school with a tray full of cookies, and gave them to the teacher, who gobbled them all up on the spot."

"Were they poisoned, Miz?"

"No. The lesson was for the teacher, 'Be sweet, be nice, and people will be nice to you.'"

"Did it work, Miz?"

"Kinda. You see he wasn't used to people being nice to him. He got indigestion and died of a heart attack the next day."

"Awesome, Miz Reims! You're totally cool!"

Two of them stole out of the room and called their grandmothers on their cell phones to see if she had a good recipe for home baked cookies. Ms Reims' stories were published, in benevolently supported magazines. For their genre they were rather good with titles such as, 'I'll never cry into Mom's Cocoa.' 'The Awesome Aliens of our Inner Space.' 'My Sister's Last Crock Pot.' But to the dismal Taff their puffball effusions couched in a collapsed form of sugarcoated verbiage, pig-Latin to his Ciceronian periods, made him want to throw up.

What cruelly jesting fate had left him foundered on these shores we do not know, and decency forbids us to enquire further. In any case when asked the same question by his colleagues, he sighed. "If only I knew. But to earn my daily crust, here I must stay."

Ms. Margaret Reims, the author of the slush driven prose was wearing one of her famous slogan emblazoned kaftans. This one proclaimed to her world. "If school sucks blow it off." A boy of thirteen was sniveling in its folds. "He gave me a C- for my homework, and I spent a good twe'nny minutes on it, honestly." When he lied he looked directly into Ms Reim's eyes so she knew he was being so truthful. "I know, honey. He's just -- well different, I suppose, than the rest of us." But under her breath she said, "Limey prick!"

What she did not know was that LP like everyone else simply wanted to be liked, but after years of harsh Welsh winters could not make that leap into the world of the warm and cuddly. When self-pity overcame him, he conjured up the image of Frankenstein's monster, tottering around the Northern Hemisphere searching for affection only to be met with revulsion and screams of horror. He had a cold Welsh schoolmaster from the Valleys soul and no amount of trying could turn that stern visage into a congenial mask. To be loved, well, he never even dreamed that, as it was so far beyond the realms of the possible. To be tolerated that would be well tolerable. No-one in the school could know just how much those averted eyes in the corridors cut him to the quick as did the muffled jeers, when he walked quickly from his room to the faculty lounge. During the bleak winter semester he hit upon an idea that would make him, if not popular, at least marginally interesting. Glancing through an adventure magazine he saw an advertisement for climbing the volcanoes of Ecuador. He invested the last of his meager savings and went off next summer to South America.

The moment of summitting Chimborazo was the happiest and most successful of his life. That night in his tent he drank a lot of water, both as a celebratory beverage, and at his instructors urging to avoid turning his blood into soup and giving him cerebral edema. An hour later the pressure in his bladder was unbearable. He had to pee, but resisted that unstoppable tide as long as a mortal could, for his tent partner, moody and unpredictable when awake, was a frightening bear when his sleep was disturbed. He unzipped the tent softly but still released a minor ice storm, which rained down on them from the condensation of their breath frozen under the tent roof, arousing his grumpy colleague. That worthy, who had not even bothered to assimilate his name, muttered, "Welsh prick!"

He slipped on his inner boots and stole out onto the carpet of ice outside the tent. The campsite was on the edge of a great sloping glacier. His smooth soled boots skated easily over its slippery surface till he found a suitable spot away from the tent. As he looked up into the star spangled heavens, framed by the cirque of great peaks, he felt alone yet at peace. 'Maybe now I will be more popular, and people will make an effort to know me.' But what he should have been thinking of was the guides warning about wandering about in the night without ice axe and crampons along the steep icy flank of a dangerous mountain.

Next morning the skid marks left by his boots made him easy to trace. When the rescue party picked his much battered body out of the crevasse two thousand feet below, they shook their heads. "Never listen, do they, assholes!" They were angry. Their jobs were at stake. A dead client's evaluation was no good to anyone.

Since he had neither friends nor relatives in the community at large, his memorial service had to be done at school. It was an awkward affair. Nobody really cared. In fact most were relieved not to have to face him and his depressing ways again. Frankly he had been a bit of a blight on the schools up-beat atmosphere. They gave him the usual eulogies, but there was no escaping their hollow sound, and giving him the best teacher award was a mistake. There were ominous rumblings from the back of the hall, the assembly zone of the 'Dudes.' To make the whole thing more palatable they wrapped it up in the normal welcome back meeting. The students stopped shuffling their feet when the ever-popular Ms Reims stepped forward to read a story. It was called, "A Day without a Hug is like a stone without a slug." In the annals of the Warm and Fuzzy Press there can have been few more sloppy pieces of maudlin drivel ever to see the light on a computer terminal, but this one brought the house down; first they chuckled, then they laughed and finally she rendered unto them her masterly peroration. "Observe the slug my sisters, and brothers. He knows the earth like the back of his shell. He lives on it and loves to hug it. So go on each of you hug like a slug." They were all in tears with joy as they each turned to hug their neighbor. "Thanks for listening to me, "she said.' You're so special and to show my appreciation for bein' so cool hearin' me out, come to my room after for brownies and cookies. The last bit she trumpeted out, while simultaneously ripping open her blouse to reveal her T-shirt underneath. "Hug me! Don't slug me!" It said. She turned around. On the back was inscribed the pithy dictum, "Kiss, don't kick!" Underneath which was an arrow pointing to the Grand Canyon of her buttocks. They all laughed; the teeny bit of sadness early on in the meeting completely forgotten.

Reg Crosses the Rio

This is a story of diversity in adversity. It may come across a mite over-cooked, especially with the hodge-podge of slang from both ends of the Atlantic, stirred into the brew, but I have to pass it on to you, or how else would you know about Reggie Ramsbotham, who for one shining moment conquered a cultural divide broader than the Big Pond itself.

Fate was doing nobody any favors the day it dealt out Reginald Ramsbotham's hand. First off, no one the right side of fifty should have to put up with being called Reginald. There was also a middle name, Rupert, which is best forgotten about, as Reggie did. To make matters worse, having a scrawny physique, from which any cannibal would be hard pressed to scrape off a bacon butty, inspired the more creative of his peers to nickname him matchstick. Political Correctness hadn't got off the ground at Nutwood Secondary Modern in the 1950s. So in 'them days,' if you stood out from the crowd in any way, and Reg suffered the double jeopardy of having a partiality for poofy stuff like Art and History, you got your head stuck down the toilet, which was their way of celebrating diversity. All in all Reggie had an unsatisfactory childhood, a fact of which he was unaware till pointed out by a very expensive therapist much later. At the time, like everyone else he just got on with it.

In early manhood, he got his lucky break. For a short spell on the road to Mr. Pickwick's face and figure, he discovered muscular development. During this butterfly period, before fading out as a dull gray moth, he took up rock-climbing. It was a curious choice, but the hills then weren't alive to the squeals and multicolored get-ups of the fashion-conscious wannabees. The sport's habitat, the permanent rain belt of Wales, The Lakes and Scotland, drew only losers, loners and oddities, while the uniform of baggy woolly breeches and monkish anoraks was enough to bring on the vapors for your dedicated follower of fashion. It was the squelchy setting together with climbing's determinedly ill clad acolytes that attracted Reggie, the sad ill-named misfit. There was another inducement. No ritualistic humiliation, in the name of the greater glory of the old school was involved, like dropping the easy catch at cricket, or the goolly crushing shots in football executed in front of a sniggering mob of ill-wishers. There was not much chance of being jeered at in a landscape peopled only by sheep and freaks. By a quirk of fate, which tailors pastimes to their patrons, he took to it like a duck to water. The low value he put on self and his preservation was a positive asset in a realm where boldness paid handsome dividends, and the skinny ugly duckling could fly.

During this gilded era, and for reasons nothing to do with this story, Reggie decided to throw caution to the winds, and decamp from the damp red-brick of his native sod, Rochdale, Lancashire, for the USA. Life was played there with more brio, than at home, where people dribbled around hunched up against the travails of existence, in a rain swept world memorialized by LS Lowry.

He managed to snare a plum job at a private university in Ohio, teaching Renaissance History. The natives thought his accent cute, and the names that had given rise to so much mirth back home, were repackaged as quaint if not lovably eccentric. Even so his best friend, a fellow boffin, Elmer Froode Ph.D., may have been selected as insurance for having a name more ridiculous than his own. Reg knew, Shakespeare not withstanding, that some roses don't smell half as sweet as others.

The funny way he talked plus his ever so polite diffidence came as a novelty-item to the Mid-West University. Girls in college bars were overheard saying, "Wow! Check out that cute accent! Doesn't it make you think of bagpipes and hairy men in skirts? You know he, like, hung out with Princess Di." His lectures began to attract a fair sprinkling of people who couldn't tell their Raphaels from their Bellinis, and thought these pictures of downcast women baring their boobies to their bare babies, weren't like the real Madonna, whose tits were like geometrical. But they were unanimous in agreeing that he was a seriously sweet cutie. Other attractions on the checklist included his self-depreciating humor, friendly grading and his heinously hairy Harris Tweeds.

Aware there was more mileage to be gained in posh talk, than in Broad Lancashire, Reggie's jettisoned his Rochdale accent faster than it took to say, "How now, brown cow." Sometimes he had a quiet chuckle to himself imagining his mates in the Old *Dog and Duck*, hearing him with his Bertie Woosterish "*I say, Old Bean*," and transparently preposterous upper-crusty airs. But in Americus, Ohio, where their only contact with Briticisms were the vicarage tea parties on Masterpiece Theater, a Queen's English, long obsolete in the sceptred Isle, was considered *bona fide*.

Melbourne van Rosendorn, of the Long Island Sound family of that name, was one girl seriously crushed on him. Melbourne, her elder brother had been dubbed Sydney, sported a deliciously buttery mop of hair, that made out her head was exploding, this together with her belladonna eyes and a chassis without a straight line ensured that she was the cynosure of the lasses in the classier sororities. No Einstein was she, but the girl knew what she wanted. Crowning her wish list was Our Reg. Him being

English therefore exotic, a professor, therefore unattainably desirable, and to an impartial eye moderately presentable, put him near the top of the 'must have' list, concocted by her *clique*, at whose very summit sat two footballing meatheads with as much conversation as your average MTV station. Having exhausted their cerebral potential very quickly, she was happy to hand them on to her cronies.

"You in a coma, Mel, babe? Never seen you this quiet. What's up?" Big Sister, Ms van Rosendorn was dishin' with her pledge mentees in the sorority common room. They were in face-packs, bath robes and cozy socks, sipping Perrier; she in a virtual reality micro-skirt needing a stretch of imagination to justify its existence, but which very effectively highlighted her willowy legs. Melbourne sighed, "See here, Marcy, I'm like seriously crushed on this totally dreamy dude." The girls stirred; this was like major news, as was anything to do with guydom. "Got it bad. I eat, sleep, go to lectures and think of nothing else. Actually I'm not eating just now, can't get to sleep, and I never go to any lectures except his.

"*He* bein' a Professor?"

"Got it in one."

"Wow! That's *molto* heinous, girl, totally funky. Keep it real, Mel, old Bud."

"I totally drool over him. Doc Reggie's he's just, like so classy. When I first saw him I was like Oh my God! *quelle* wierdo accent, 'Ta-ra, luv, fancy a cuppa?'" Here she made a fairish imitation of, did she but know it, George Formby, a Lancashire comedian of bygone days. "I could listen to him all day. His accent totally rules, and that old world sophistication!" Melbourne had only a sketchy idea of the labyrinthal complexities of the English Class System."

"OK sister, what's this hottie like?"

A dreamy expression came over Melbourne, "He's tall, well taller than me. Distinguished and tweedy, real tweedy, leather patches on elbows, that sort of thing."

"Hair? Any?"

"Still plenty; dark, parted in the middle can you believe that? Sort of Cary Grant in dialect."

"Like *who?*"

She ignored this, "Not great looking actually, sort of ordinary, till when he opens his mouth. Great smile, but English teeth."

"So? You getting it on, girl?"

"No way, I'm so totally failing."

"Not like you."

"No. Well let's say it's a long-term assignment, a semester project."

"Well, ok, what gives?"

"I sit right in front of him at his lectures and give him the treatment."

"Like staring him with those baby blue, eyes?"

"Like that and ...More like ...proactive than that."

"Proactive? Where you comin' from, girl? Sure you not sleepin' with *some* prof-dude, Mel?"

"Well like I was sayin' I was proactive, like one day when he was doing the Italian Renaissance, I tried to doll myself up, like, you know, what I thought a Perugino angel looked like."

"Wings?" Melbourne delivered the impudent freshman, what used to be called a withering look. "No, but I did wrap myself in a clean sheet. Next time I dressed as one of Botticelli's Three Graces. I was going to make a big splash as Venus rising from the waves, until someone told me she came out bare-assed. I totally wasn't ready for that. Even so wearing a see through nightie in the middle of November, man! Did I freeze my butt off for love! Anyhow for the mid-term review session I went as Mona Lisa, holding that funny smile till my face ached."

"Wow! Way to go, girl. Did it work? Did he notice?"

"No. I might as well *of* gone shopping."

Actually Reggie did notice this extraordinarily pretty girl, who always sat right in front of the class, dressed in Halloween costume, pulling funny faces at him, and wondered what he had done to attract such wierdos.

"So how come you fell for Limey Lover Boy?"

"You really, totally, want to know?" A bevy of big hairdos nodded as one. "It's so like embarrassing. We were in his Western Civ Seminar checking him out. I was like going off about Hitler, and how he invaded Australia. I mean Austria, Australia, what's the big deal? But I was making a total jerk of myself, with everyone trying not to laugh, when this major geek asked how The Big H fought off the kangaroos. They all just about collapsed with laughter. 'My bad.' I said, trying to recover, but they went on howling. I so wanted to die. I was, like, almost crying, when Doc Ramsbotham smoothed things over with a joke, 'Did we know, there was an Hell of a difference between the two?'"

"Eh?"

"Austria and Australia. Like 'L' of a difference."

The girls exchanged surreptitious looks. Mel was taking education seriously?

Thus was Melbourne bowled over with the warmth of his charm, like the sun breaking through a cloudburst in Rochdale. After this she adored him with the devotion of the true disciple. In her innocence she would gaze up at Reg with a purity of expression of a Michelangelo Sibyl. She was, however, a child of her time....

"You know I always get 'em in the end. Yep I'm goin' to snatch that Limey hottie and see what these stiff upper lips are made of." Romance with a capital 'R' was not yet dead in Ohio. But being in love is the least contagious of afflictions, and her uninfected buddies shook their heads wondering about the shelf life of this romance, and whispered, "The guy is like majorly unhunky. I give it a week," Then sped off to tackle the now-freed-up meatheads.

But snatch him she did. Recognizing from clues that climbing was a *sine qua non* to pluck this chicken, Melbourne took lessons, and mugged up on mountain books to be at least on nodding terms with the game's esoteric lingo. Much to the surprise of Melbourne's cheerleading chums she found she liked it, and didn't have to feign those orgasmic shrieks when lowered to the deck after a more than normally exciting vertical experience. She had caught the bug, and even thrilled to the master's stories of gripping epics on desperate climbs.

Now with the hunt for Reg running on full steam, Melbourne spent an age getting dolled up for the gym for G (Grab the Guy)-Day. Dominating her ensemble was a tight fitting burgundy bralette tank, with the enigmatic inscription, 'I climb a crock' (*sic*). Burgundy Lycra climbing shorts meshed in nicely. Completing her outfit were her burgundy rock shoes, a velvet burgundy chalk bag, and with her big hair neatly corralled by a white silk Alice band to match her chalky hands, her get up was impeccable.

Reg was in the midst of his warm up stretches, when she sauntered up, nice and casual like, her perfume giving advance warning of her presence; a zedoary laden zephyr. "Excuse me, can you, like, hold my rope, while I take a ride on this?"

"No problemo."

She had practiced this route many, many times, and so with a flick of her magnificent mane, a come hither look in her eyes and a posterior sculpted by Praxiteles, she scampered up easily.

"Nice Job." Reg was impressed.

"Thanks." And, "Hey. If your partner's not here, we could climb together?" She sounded almost nonchalant.

"Sounds good." He wondered why he was the chosen one when the gym was heaving with Sylvester Stallone look-alikes.

Later at TGI Fridays, the lady, having steered him into buying her one of these lethal cocktails disguised as a fruit basket, put him in the picture. He looked with interest at the girl over the frothy beer like concoction currently frosting his mouth like Novocain. At first he thought she was seventeen, but now saw she was in her early twenties. He surmised she must have got hold of an elixir that stuck her in high school for eternity. "I've seen you before." She smiled with a set of perfect white teeth that Rochdale could never match. "I'm in your class." Then it dawned on him, this was all set up. Before he could say, 'If you'll excuse me, I have papers to grade,' Melbourne started, "Now that problem you were telling us about, the identity of the Delphic Sibyl in the Sistine, I believe you said..." She stuck her left elbow on the bar right in his face. At first he thought she was challenging him to a bout of arm wrestling. Then it clicked. She was imitating of the pose of the Delphic Sibyl! The trap was sprung, for that was who she, sort of, vaguely, in the right light, looked like, the living breathing embodiment of the lady decorating the roof of the Sistine Chapel.

From there it wasn't a long haul for the lady to brief him thoroughly, although difficult to catch for the normal din was over laden by cell phone conversations competing for air space. "Again, please," asked Reg and in the end, she had to shout her declaration of intent above the hub-ub. Despite recognizing this as a defining moment in a career, not so far strewn with broken hearts or hymens, he was stumped. Why would such a babe want to associate with him? Recovering, he answered the amazing proposition, "I say, steady on, old girl. Rather!" Not a hill of beans *apropos* meaning, but Melbourne went all a-flutter, hearing a patois unheard since the old Indian Raj folded the flag and retired to Bournemouth.

In less time than it takes to make Beijing Duck, the May and late September twosome were officially an item. In a town noted for its plenitude of fooderies Reg found himself squiring her to top-end eateries. For a lad from Lancashire, where a night out consisted of a rake of pints at' Nags Head, a suicide curry to follow, with a Grande Finale puking over dad's geraniums, it was all a bit dizzying, and hair-raisingly expensive. Sometimes he had to pinch himself, "Am I really dating a Homecoming-Queen with big hair?" And when he really couldn't believe his luck, he wondered, "Am I going to wake up sad, lonely and it's raining in Rochdale?"

There was one, "But only if..." from the lady. "I say, Reggie, Old Boy,"- she wasn't altogether humorless. "Do you want to prove you're like my serious sweetie, doing something heinously amazing to win this ole gal, *a la* James Bond? That climb you're always on about? Wha's-a-name? Double O-Seven, you know, at Seneca. Take me up that, baby, and collect your booty."

"Oh, rather! But you mean Triple S... I think, and hope not."

"Yea, same difference. Take me.... like up *Triple S*, Reggie."

"Flippin' Nora!" dropping the tone of his speech a social register or two, Reggie remembered she was a little Princess used to getting her way with anyone a generation further up the line than her.

"I'm gonna hold you to your promise. You said you'd take me there first decent weekend. Remember? Well first decent weekend's comin' up. Remember telling me about the joint." Here her voice went into that flutey upper register oft used to mock Transatlantic Cousins. "Seneca, a slice of a vanished America captured in perpetuity by Norman Rockwell, a Brigadoon forever frozen in the fifties, a world lost to developers and the Mickey Mouse Syndrome that commonly blights the American landscape." Incorporated into the libretto was an exaggerated posturing of the posterior plus an intermezzo of fluttering gesticulations of hand and eye.

"Yes it's a super spot, but America's Cenotaph Corner?" Reggie stuttered in alarm, for the route and its Welsh counterpart had a horrendous reputation. Then calming down, "Rather! A jolly old caper, what? But would Mallory approve?" he added cannily.

"So who's this Mallory, dude? What's it to him?"

"Well...Some believe he was the first up Everest. He disappeared into the fog way high up. Never seen again. Many want to believe it. He climbed, 'Because it's there.' The purist ideal, the Golden Rule. There's no other possible motivation for mountaineering."

"Doc. Ramsbotham, that's awesomely cool, but I so seriously want to climb it. Don't you? It's *my* Everest, Reggie dude. Don't you want to lead me there? Like, you know, Virgil leading Dante through Heaven and Hell. Remember?"

How could any red-blooded American, even if he were English, refuse such a plea, especially when it was accompanied by eyes the size of Mocha-cups and pearly little tears edging their way over her cheekbones.

"Well?"

"Couldn't we do Ecstasy Junior instead?" This fine climb was a scamper in comparison.

"Doc Ram... Reggie baby, don't you get it? It's Triple S, and you're Triple R, Reginald Rupert Ramsbotham and R comes before S in the alphabet. As for the other *Ecstasy* thingy that for afters, if you're a good boy." This was the first intimation the relationship had carnal potential.

"Ah, yes. I should cocoa." She stared bemused. "That means I get it." Reg still wasn't with the algebra, but saw it was the Three S'es climb or nowt, if he wanted to claim that much sought after pound or two of flesh.

What caused her to put such a high premium on a glorified roll in the hay? Melbourne, an indefatigable church-sampler amidst the *potpourri* of Christian denominations on offer, was a born again virgin. In answer to her pastor's call she had taken a vow of chastity to unleash the power of maidenheads against a national conspiracy of pornographic, and sexually harassing Satanists. She never encountered any problems finding boy friends, so, unlike many of her generation, never felt compelled to drop the drawbridge to be in the popular crowd. Melbourne reckoned if her knight-errant, Reggie, was willing to demonstrate his commitment by taking on this mission, then she would be willing to split the difference and allow him entrance into Paradise Garden.

Others would commit a drive-by-shooting for such a girlfriend, but her stance as a virgin for Jesus, imposed such a strain on Old Reg that after every frustrated date he limped home, to the joyless relief of the old fashioned hand pump. Anyway it would be churlish to turn the lady down. The reader will not approve; Mallory would not have approved, but then he wouldn't have approved of much that went under the name of mountaineering nowadays.

The weekend was set up with great finesse. A trip down in his new turbo convertible-he had got some serious wheels now- fish-tailing round the bends at hair-raising speed to get the glands glowing. Two separate tents pitched far apart to ensure no randy romps in the night for the pledged twosome before the ritual consecration, security being backed up with the double indemnity of a lock down zipper on the lady's flysheet. A couple of good stiff climbs to build up anticipation, followed by a wholesome dip in the swimming hole, more tingling flesh, then early to bed, a hearty breakfast, and celebratory photos from the summit, to verify the ascent. A candlelit dinner was arranged in Harper's Country Restaurant. Melbourne's flirty frock a knock-off of Gwyneth Paltrow's Oscar gear, with matching pink champagne and pepperoni pizza, was chosen to coordinate with the sunset over Seneca. Completion of contract to follow in the Oakum Motel. In his imagination he could see her spread out on the bed, a bottle of California Asti-Spumante in the fridge, and who knows where it would go from there.

On the way down they saw the West Virginia Motto, on a billboard Reg read "'Montani semper Liberi.' They think it means, 'mountaineers are always free,' but it's really 'Mountaineers are always children.'"

"I knew that." Melbourne tended to be on the defensive after the Austria/ Australia debacle. Reg chuckled, "They may have a point."

"How so?"

"Oh, never mind." For another intellectual challenge was in the offing as a quatrain of signs came rushing at them in rhyming couplets, spaced many yards apart, for the slow reader or the fast driver.

"My mom sleeps safe

She has no fear

And it's because

Her gun is near."

This ditty apparently composed by the hitherto unsung loiterer in Parnassus, notgunshy.com, added to Reg's checklist of worries. Having what he considered a mature European take on the Second Amendment, he steered well clear from any fire-arms. If even the moms of America had to keep revolvers where they normally stowed their nighties Reg could easily be accused of irresponsibility bringing a lass out here unarmed. Worrying about what to do if faced with a pistol-packing momma took his attention off the road for that crucial instant.

It was the hairpin bend after Elkins. The car skidded on a patch of oil, slewing wildly out of control. Then the front tire blew, and for one horrific moment they were hurtling toward the cliff edge. Melbourne screamed, her hormones zinging prematurely. One of the wheels touched air. Reg hauling desperately at the steering just managed to pull the machine back from the abyss. They ground to a halt, shaken but uninjured. Melbourne's enthusiasm for the venture, was sort of muted. "I'm frightened Doc R. I don't know if I'm cut out for this kinda thing. Are we nearly there, already?"

"Yep! But this'll take a while." And when she started to cry, Reg got flustered. "Sorry, luv, I'm doing my best." You see, despite everything she really was just a kid. It started to rain so Reg changed the tire as fast as he could. But it came hammering down flattening Melbourne's tresses.

"My hair!' she wailed, "Look at my hair, Doc." Reg looked, and saw the leonine mane tamed into a sorry rat-tailed mop. He had never seen her before without an extensive preparatory toilette, and for the first time the magic temporarily abated. She seemed kind of dull.

"What am I doing in this Loser-ville dump?" She lit a cigarette savagely; her hands shaking so much several matches had to be sacrificed. This was the first Reg knew she smoked. Her desirability quotient dropped another inch or two. Melbourne's belief in Reg's infallibility also took a bit of a battering. She was of the school that said, 'Your crash, your fault,' but then she had yet to get her first bumper dent. Here was the first crack in the gilded stucco.

Melbourne's good humor restored by some chilled red wine, helped make pitching the tents, normally an onerous task, frolicsome, with much jostling and bottom bumping in the dark. The rain had stopped as suddenly as it had begun, leaving everything cleaner. Fronds of mist withering away in the night sky revealed a casket of stars glistening overhead. Reg called, "See, Melbourne, shooting stars," as they whooshed silently across the heavens. "That's us," he whispered wistfully. "Sure," she said, but her eyes sparkled like she wanted to believe, and on that rising tide of excitement, a promissory note was exchanged in the form of a long rapturous kiss, followed by the regretful sound of tents zipping as they went separately to bed.

The smell of roast coffee and bacon sizzling on the grill were the first sensations to greet Reg next morning. Often accused of being a spoilt Princess, Melbourne, morale boosted by a complete cosmetic makeover, was merrily playing the 'Little Woman.' Life couldn't be bettered.

"Ecce Thump, I could murder' cuppa cocoa," struck the wrong chord for the Golden Girl, since *coffee* was merrily bubbling away on the percolator. But it was something else that shook her composure, as the Thing from the Depths crawled out of the tent, eyes unfocused, hair askew, something awful dangling from nostrils which on closer inspection turned out to be a clump of sleeping-bag feathers. Melbourne, insulated from horrid reality, had never seen the male first thing in the morning, man at his most bestial, definitely not the moment to catch Reggie at his prime. Why he had suddenly reverted to plebian mode, Goodness knows. There was something horribly gross about that accent, that didn't jibe with her picture of the English Knight. 'And Oh my God! Cocoa! Did anyone under ninety drink the stuff?' Melbourne had visions of her gran slurping the muddy mixture while hunting for her teeth, and now that Reg was grinning toothily at her with his full frontal exhibit of European dental malpractice, like a row of broken Dolomite peaks, Melbourne was like; 'Oh my God!'

As they stepped out from the parking lot a swarthy Adonis roared up on an ultra-phallic motor-bike, gazed hungrily at Melbourne, and then revving up unnecessarily, managed to fit into his schedule a sneer at Reg's Saab, the car for the middle-aged at heart. From Mohican crop down to his Gucci cowboy boots the stubbly Greek god was a tribute to trend. He stared fiercely at the lass, as would a lion summoning his lioness to the water hole. She couldn't but compare the Dark Man's animal summons to Reg's cocoa call. First impressions do count.

Plodding the steep zigzags to the crag, Reg pointed out items of interest. Having climbed Cenotaph Corner back home, no sweat -or so he recollected- Reggie's thoughts were focused festively on the evening ahead rather than the climb, itself, a fatal error. Those stressful moments on his first assault of the Corner, when after ages of knackered pull-ups on fixed gear, he peeled off halfway up, had long been locked away in Memory Lane. This Yankee cousin would give no problem, he reckoned, catching a glimpse of himself in his mind's eye styling upwards, gliding over crux and bulge, as might a medieval saint levitate.

Rabbits ran across their path, underscoring the bucolic nature of their adventure. Sweet Cecily lay by the trail, close by was a yellow Lizard's Tail, whose cone-shaped flower curved and dwindled till it tapered off into sweet nothings. Adding to the ambiance, a cardinal twittered merrily, while a luminous black butterfly fluttered by the couple, the dappled forest light capturing its silken texture for a splendid ephemeral moment.

To all the flora and fauna assembled for her gratification, Melbourne could only offer non-committal, half-hearted monosyllables, and now and then a listless *awesome*. Where, where was the leg kicking gusto expected from a cheerleader of a Big-Ten School?

"Awesome," she muttered absently. But her indifferent 'Wows!' her diffident, 'Oh, Cools!' and distracted "Phatts!' did not signal a flagging zest for the Englishman. The steep walk had so totally shagged her out, that half-hearted hurrahs were all her lungs allowed. Melbourne, as physically flawless as they come, was totally unprepared for the rigors of the mountain.

They reached the base of the climb.

"We'll rest here."

"Reggie, baby, that's the first sensible thing you've said all day." She tousled his hair affectionately. You see, she really liked him despite the astronomical differences in age and habitat.

Although there were a few blemishes round the fringes of her infatuation, she still carried in her heart the desire to be swept away by the mysterious Englishman. She couldn't wait for the apotheosis of emotion when they emerged triumphant from their quest. She would submit under the stars with the music of the spheres egging them on. Yet in her heart of hearts she wanted him packaged with the sexy motorbike, now thrumming up and down the valley under the brutal hunk, with the lax shaving schedule. Anyway when bodily fluids had been exchanged in solemn covenant, she would prevail upon him to ditch his mid-life-crisis Saab and get with it on a Harley. As for his clothes, where else was a woman duty's, but to burn his tweeds, then steer her man mallside, to check out some serious threads.

Reg dumped the gear at the foot of the corner, looked up and got a fright. Gone were the accommodating ledges, the comforting crack and colossal jugs he had stormed up in his dreams. A quick glance at the smooth, evilly impending dierdre brought him back to earth with a start. If Reg needed to impress, it would have been better to go for a route already wired, and not be stretching sweaty, chalk-smeared fingers out into the unknown. Put not such trust in Cupid. He was scared stiff, hands clammy, throat dry, a tic started to tap his right cheek, and in his stomach he felt a sour lump of lead. He gazed at the route, wondering how anyone could get up this hundred feet of holdless verticality. He had a fleeting nostalgic cast at life's gentler pleasures, and decided he wanted to play golf, even though he had never given it or its participants the time of day before. Now the sudden allure of the game made him replan his life. He would borrow clubs, sneak onto a course, half-way round, and sod the penalties for this little piece of sharp practice, which were as nothing compared to the business facing him. All life's pastimes and pleasures, in fact all life itself were wrapped up in the pointless assault of this chunk of malignant, unremitting granite.

"Bring it on, man!" What did she mean? Best not to ask just now. Reg uncoiled the rope, sorting out the gear rack with stumbling fingers, and then started up the corner. As soon as hands and feet touched rock he knew it was no-go. Mentally he wasn't psyched up properly. He had been too relaxed, and without stage fright you flopped. Now fear engulfed him in great numbing surges. A proper lemon he felt, an unarticulated lemon, a broken stringed puppet. From experience Reggie knew he should call it quits. He couldn't get up nor could he give up. He tried to style but as in dreams when you try to run, his limbs wouldn't play. Exerting some elbow grease, he hauled himself up a few feet, arms straining and feet trembling. Sweaty hands, turning the chalk into clay, slithered about on diminutive holds. He scrabbled through his rack; wires and slings snagging everywhere, feverishly trying to find some protection. At last! A runner came off the belt. He slung it into the crack anyhow. It refused to fit. Shakily Reg reversed a few feet, then frutching upwards grimly, he managed to seat the piece properly, but now was totally blown. "Give it your best shot, Reggie, boy!" this was Mel through gritted teeth, it now dawning on her that the ascent wasn't going to be the advertised cinch. He slithered back a few feet, and then bumbled up to thread the rope; his breath coming out fast and heavy. A few gasps to collect himself for this desperate game of vertical chess, then sensing Melbourne getting impatient, he moved tremulously. "Jesus wept!" Panting like a knackered dog, Reg thrashed his way up to what seemed a resting position. But there was nothing there. He looked down, 'Christ Almighty!' He was way, way above his last piece of protection. If he fell, he'd hit the ground, making a hell of a mess. His arms solid with lactic acid couldn't hold much longer. A crack appeared in front of his nose. Furiously he snatched a protective runner off his rack, forcing it into the crack. Quick! Clip! 'Thank you, Lord!' It held.

"Mel, hold rope tight will you?" He grabbed the runner. "No! Pull real tight!" The rope slid ever so slightly. "Haul! C'mon for Christ's sake HURRY!" Then the piece shifted. Reg shrieked so loud it could be heard in his pub back home, which was exactly where he wished he were now.

He managed another few feet up the crack, but every move felt like a swimmer swept into shark-infested waters. Another runner provided temporary refuge. This segment of the route went slightly out of the crack. Reg knew he hadn't an earthly of getting up, even in the gym it would be beyond his reach. Here with nothing but air beneath his feet he froze. The more he tried the more he knew he was done. Defeat, and tonight would be canceled, so delaying the inevitable, he hung on, tiring himself more. A feeble sally was attempted, laybacking up an inch or two, feet skidding, and hand over sweaty hand slipping in the crack. He rabbited back down, hanging shamelessly onto the rope.

So there was Reg, hoisted by the petard of his ego, stranded too many feet above the last ill-placed runner, with squashy bananas fingers, and legs beginning that slow cycling slither that preludes saying good-bye to the rock. He was hanging on, his feet spinning in the air. "Oh, bollocks. I'll have to move now, else I'm off." He made a frantic lunge at a hand jam. "Gordon Bennett! If I can only get fingers in't bleedin' crack." His fingers gave way without warning. "Shit!" He was off, screaming through space, one runner ripping after another. 'The whole bloody lot is unzipping!' He stopped suddenly, one tiny camming device holding him, still bobbing up and down, a white-faced Melbourne grimly gripping the rope. Meanwhile, the motor-biking Adonis popped up from nowhere, to lie on a boulder beside Melbourne, and sneer languidly in the sunshine.

"*Quelle* Bummer! You're so in the shit, man," observed the perceptive fellow. "Like you got Teflon soles on your shoes, Homey."

After handing out these useful insights he strolled over to the foot of the climb, and stood there savoring the awareness of his uebermensch presence. Melbourne her fear gone, let her eyes roam over his magnificent physique. He noticed, and satisfied that the chick was of acceptable standard for the employment of his obelisk like tadger, flexed his biceps, easily accessible to view under his muscle shirt. The rest of his muscular frame rippled to and fro like a breeze blowing over a duck pond. "It's a cruise, man," he shouted up unhelpfully. "Sod this!" said Reg, kissing good-bye to Bertie Wooster voice-overs. "Lower me down, Sweetie." Melbourne glowered, and lowered letting the big guy assist with the rope handling.

"What's your name, Hun, Bun?"

"Melbourne. Yours?"

"Jake, but call me Iceman...Melbourne."

"OK. Iceman Jake. Right pleased to make your acquaintance," she replied coyly.

"Likewise."

The left out Reg was unceremoniously lowered to the deck. If the horrible truth be told a sack of potatoes had more grace than our sad sportsman. "Uncool, man," Iceman pronounced. Then, "Want me rescue your cam?"

The camming device was a very expensive piece of equipment. "Yea," said Reg humbly. He knew enough not to say, 'please.' What else was there for him to do?

Iceman Jake took the gear from Reg's shoulders, as if he were removing the regalia of a deposed monarch. Then he uncoiled the rope, flicking it round his neck to keep his coiffure out of the loops. "Man, you were way above yourself," says he, before passing on a brilliant smile to Melbourne. Jake Man whipped on a flash pair of rock boots, dusted his hands lightly with chalk, then nodded to Melbourne. "On Belay, Hun, Bun?"

"Belay on, Jake"

"Climbing."

"Climb on,"

Off he romped, styling like Reg in his dreams. Every so often the upward momentum was halted to slip in minimalist protection, sneer at Reg and smile hunkily at Melbourne. Reg expected he would ignore the jammed cam, and stroll on, but he clipped in ever so casually before continuing. Annoyingly at the point where Reg met his Waterloo, the Rock God skipped and danced with ease.

"You were nowhere near the crux," said Jake helpfully. "Off belay!" There he was at the top smug as a bug.

"Takin' in."

"That's me."

"OK, C'mon up. You'll cream it, babe. Cakewalk. You go, girl!"

Melbourne started rather tremulously, but then gained confidence. With the Rock-Meister at the helm, she moved smoothly upward, the continuous motion only broken by the twosome trading what seemed to be mortal insults.

"You Bitchin' babe You kick ass!"

"Man, You smoked that, you bad ass, man!"

But the effect was the opposite. Judging by the intimacy of their smiles each sally bonded the fabulous couple closer. It was akin to a Masonic ritual for which Reg had neither key nor password. Dimly, he perceived that even if he grew a hairy chest he would never gain admittance. He knew this but he would never know why, for this was the great question the eternal loser has pondered throughout the ages.

"Hun, Bun, you totally rule." Jake was impressed.

The gear, except for Reggie's Friend, came out easily. Mel pushed, pulled and swore, tearing her hand on the rock, before she freed it. The Ice-man sternly shook his head, "Bummer placement, dude, you gotta learn to put your thing in right, specially when a girl's involved." Melbourne chucked the piece at Reg, her beautiful face contorted with contempt. Mere words could not begin to cope with all the disdain, derision, and finality she put into this gesture, and she had ascended without a slip, nor an urgent call for a tight rope.

"You were like totally sucky, Reggie, Boy!" Disillusionment is shattering. Perceptions unravel so finally, as when you see mummy kissing Santa Claus, who just happens to be Your Uncle Fred, or when an idol falls off his perch and all the king's horses and all the king's men can't put him back up there again.

On that note the lady's interest in our hero faded forever. Reg was left to witness the smile that flashed between the two Olympians, and in that instant when her face lit up with a beauty that made him ache to his boots, it struck a melancholy reminder of all those things in life that would forever pass him by.

Just before Melbourne disappeared that night with Iceman Jake, she made her good-byes. "You blew it, Old Limey Bean. So go screw yourself, cos this chick won't be doin' it for you," putting Reg in the picture with admirable clarity. From Mr. Chips to Mr. Sucks all in the course of a day's work. To understand the impact of the change that came over her, on Doctor Ramsbotham Ph.D., Eccles Hand Loom Weaving College, author of the magisterial, *Variations on the Spinning Jenny in use in Rochdale during the French Revolution*, imagine, if you can, one of Jane Austen's gals flipping Mr. Darcy the bird and you have the picture.

It guttered down all night and all next morning, leaving the campsite like the Somme on a bad day in 1916. Word must have got around, for no one spoke to him, as he sludged around in the mud. He drove off aimlessly, finally stopping exhausted at an anonymous dumpy town on the Ohio River, whose bloom had already faded when Sherman paid a visit.

Maybe the local populace weren't hearing too well that night. Whenever he stopped to ask the way, people stood frozen in their tracks, staring at him like he was speaking Cherokee. As soon as he moved away conversation resumed its normal hum, as if the uncomfortable novelty of the outside world could be switched off, just as a bad programme on the Telly.

Every restaurant, bar and fast foodery was packed out with boisterous Hell's Angels, whose convention had just hit town. Everyone was having a good time except him, jeering, singing, getting wasted or just riding up and down the streets, all beards, bellies and Nazi Storm-Trooper helmets, horns tooting and engines malignantly farting. He turned a quiet corner, at the end of which a miniature pagoda, kitted out with tiny bells, paper dragons and lanterns solemnly swaying in the breeze, was gently chiming. It was the Temple of Heavenly Peace; just what he needed. The restaurant, when he entered, was empty, which should have warned him. Mandarins and lesser bowing minions ushered him to a table tucked in a murky alcove chock-a-bloc with yellowed paintings and jaded relics of the Ming Dynasty. Smiling inscrutably they dished up greasy chunks of glazed pork that slid down the gullet easily, but were to lie ticking in his stomach like glutinous time-bombs. It wasn't what had he wanted but he was too pissed off to bother explaining. So he swallowed and heard the opening salvo of battle in his innards. More glum than ever, Reggie left a stingy tip. The old waiter used to discourtesy from the natives, bowed him out, inscrutable to the last.

Cannonades of indigestible pork were bombarding his stomach lining, as he trudged around the crowded town. Everything, everywhere seemed to be designed to get on his nerves. Brassed off with it all he started back to the campsite, forgetting his silly pink hat, a nerd marker, if there ever was one. This was easily recognized by the car load of red-necks plus fluff chicks, which pulled up opposite. Reg was too good a target to pass unremarked. "Hey fairy. Wanna a fun time tonight?" This query provoked a paroxysm of laughter. "Hey, wienerhead, what you gonna do? Where'd you get that hat, homey?" So it was Saturday night. They were having fun. He slunk on, smarting, trying to shut them out; the pink hat a badge of the slinker. Passers-by stood back for his passage of shame. The braying and hooting increased, "Hey, Bubby-Sue, looks like he ain't even got no weeny wiener." The lady to whom this *bon mot* was addressed screamed with laughter. His face matching his pink cap Reg's cup of humiliation runneth over. To be laughed at by a woman, that was it; the dam of anger welling up inside him suddenly exploded.

All the frustration, mortification and indigestion of the last twenty-four hours rose up in rebellion inside him. The polite mild-mannered Englishman was gone. One look at this flotsam of American Youth Culture, with their angry tattoos, sweaty muscle shirts, and ramshackle car, told him, any reasoned request was a waste of breath. Forget the civilised, "I say, chaps. Can't a fellow enjoy his evening stroll in peace?" A Churchillian bulldog, pulsating with rage stalked resolutely towards the car. Meanwhile the sensible portion of his brain was hammering on the inside of his skull, screaming, "What the Bloody Hell are you doing? Walk away, you mad fool! For Christ's sake, forget it!" But the mad fool had taken over, and his legs just kept right on walking, independent of any rational thought.

He stepped up to the driver's side. The four hoodlums and their girls, perhaps having run out of interesting things to say, were silent. If one of them had been the red-blooded all-American male of legend, Reg would be road-kill. In a final nod to Britannia, Reg gave the classic two-fingered V salutation, with its overtones of Agincourt, and in this mood of careless rapture wiped his fingers, still greasy from the sweet and sour pork, over the loud lout's face.

"Listen, You Mo'ffing assholes! Got your brains up your butts?" He had made the trip across the Atlantic. Sure, he was too late to get a decent berth on the Mayflower, but he was here on the coat-tails of the last arrival on Ellis Island. Suddenly he had become an American in thought, word and deed. To celebrate his shining moment, he adapted his fingers to the American mode of offence and rammed the prescribed digit into the culprit's mouth so that he too might share his dining experience. It cleaned his finger but was not altogether a wise thing to do, as the hooligan could easily have bitten it off, but he just sat like a baby with its dummy, too shit scared to do anything.

The other finger he wiped off down the front of the girl-friend's T-Shirt, surreptitiously enjoying the traverse of bump and valley, cashing in on the erotic moment, he had missed out on earlier. He felt no shame at his ungallantry, but thought the ashen-faced girl might not have shared the thrill.

Embarrassment gripped the car in an unexpected frost. Reg had ruined their evening. No-one would get laid in that old jalopy tonight. He thought of kicking the said vehicle, to round off the evening, but no that was illegal, and besides he might stub his toe.

As Reg walked away, from the scene of his triumph, he assumed the rolling, "I own the world and Texas too," stride of the confident American. The prissy, sphincter fixated English gait was forever expunged. He had made the cultural exchange, crossed the Rio Grande and emerged safely on the other side. Best of all, for one sweet moment he knew how John Wayne felt every day of his life.

A few drops of rain spotted the road, forecasting the onset of a light drizzle. Then he remembered, in this land of extremes, there was no midway between torrential rain or drought. There's nothing worse than pitching a tent in the wet, so Reg ran off to set up camp before it got soaked.

We Never Knew Her Name

It was just a matter of time.

"There it is!" The other three leapt forward running through the snow to the head of the corrie, little white puff balls spurting off their heels. I had no illusions, so I walked slowly, bracing myself for what lay ahead.

They were standing around the body in a dither of indecision. It didn't need more than a glance to tell me that whoever it was, was dead. "It's a woman." Brian broke the silence, and I realized, I knew who it was.

This was a long time ago, when climbing was very different. We were all disciples of the works of WH Murray, whose two volumes arrived as if with our mothers' milk. Rock climbing, ice climbing, and hill walking were all building blocks, all vital, all of equal weight in the grand collective experience we called mountaineering, which had a lot to do with the romance and poetry of the outdoors and nothing to do with the world of designer labels. Isolation was the ideal; the frenetic proximity of the gym anathema. If there were any who didn't take off their PA's in September to pad around the hills, brilliant in their Pre-Raphaelite Autumnal colors, in bendy boots, I had never heard of them. As to the affair itself, nowadays you would call it a learning experience like Whymper's descent of the Matterhorn was a learning experience.

Our base this weekend was Jean's Hut, at that time located somewhere in the bog land below Coire Cas on the Rothiemurchus side of the Cairngorms. To call the hut a hovel was like saying your semi-detached bungalow in Duddingston was Holyrood Palace, but the word has not yet been invented to do justice to the charmless nastiness of this rustic slum. Mind you, it had the advantage that its freezing squalor guaranteed that there would be no competition for bed space. The door couldn't be shut as, a whale-back of snow had forced it open and unbidden pushed its way into the centre of the room bringing with it unseasonable air-conditioning. We must have managed some sleep in this midden, for the skier banging at the door complained he had been knocking some time.

"Youse seen a wimmin here?"

"No?" I was still baffled by sleep, and couldn't figure out what he was asking or hinting at. This was not the sort of question generally expected for climbers huddled in a horrible igloo, hardly your ideal assignation location. Then, when he told us that a woman had been wandering about all night looking for her companion, we cottoned on. "There's a search party out here looking for her."

"You won't be needing our help, then?" I said this in the tone I used for discouraging unwanted doorstep salesmen. There was a blizzard banging away outside and I had no interest in swapping my warm pit for its discomfort "You seem to have loads of volunteers." Outside I caught glimpses in momentary breaks in the swirling snow of a long queue of skiers lined up earnestly prodding the snow with their poles. Although, for all the good they were doing, they might as well be searching for Roman coins. The terrain was flat, occasionally sloping but not even as steeply as a bunker on Swanston Golf Course. Brian leaped out of bed as if scalded. "Of course we're going!" He said chiding me for my chicken-heartedness and him representing the selfless tradition of the Hillman going to the aid of his fellow climber in distress.

When we finally got ourselves outside, the skiers were still there, patiently pricking out needles in haystacks on the gentle ski slope of Coire Cas. Adding to their number was pointless, so we crossed the ridge into Coire An Sneachda where there were real cliffs to fall over. On our way we picked up two English lads, plodding through the porridge like snow towards some route on Aladdin's Buttress, who immediately volunteered to join the search.

Both Robertson and I were still pretty green. Most of our experience was second hand, a combination of reading Mountaineering in Scotland and Nanga Parbat Pilgrimage, making for a volatile mixture. We were still boys, really, products of Edinburgh public schools, with the arrogance of callow youths who thought we were God's gift to wherever we might presume to donate our talents. That weekend was to give our presumptions a stinging rebuke no schoolmaster could deliver.

It was to be our first excursion into the realm of the ice climb. We had howked our way up Ben Lui's Centre Couloir and other venerated snow bound classics in the canon, religiously following in the footsteps of the Grand Old Masters, even to the extent of wearing tricouni nailed boots. This was different. Far less hospitable than the west was the Cairngorm climate with frigid gales whipping across the Arctic plateau; added to which vertical ice was an unyielding and unforgiving medium compared to ice axe friendly snow.

We were tackling the Vent, a grade III winter climb tucked in the left hand fold of Stob Coire an Lochan. Its ice-pitch, elementary to the expert was loaded with traps for the novice. That rock up there, sticking up like a volcanic island in a frozen sea, which looked as if it was sporting an accommodating jughandle, was ice-coated, and the snow patch, yonder luring you on to a safe haven was a treacherous sugary smear coated over the ice.

It was also the first time out using crampons. The man in Lilywhites assured me they were a perfect fit, despite the two front drop spikes sticking out a good half inch from the toe of my boot, which fell off on any excursion exceeding ten yards. My fault in not strapping them on properly, the salesman told me, like he knew and I was an idiot, when he told me to pull the straps tight enough to guarantee frostbite.

The only way up ice was by step-cutting, every upward move was strenuous demanding a modicum of subtle craftsmanship. If you tried to skip a few steps, hoping to levitate to the top of the pitch, you could expect trouble. The belays weren't too hot either, a belief in prayer was as effective as an ice-axe stuck in the snow, and as for running belays, good luck. Measured against the march of technology, we were at the rubbing two sticks together stage. Ice pegs were superannuated tent pegs from Bertram Mills Circus, hard to insert, requiring a dentist's tenacity to extract, and they didn't come with a guarantee of arresting a fall. Over spiky rocks we could drape a sling, and that was that. Stories, filtering up from down south, of nuts purloined from railway sleepers jammed in cracks as runners, were taken as another example of the Sassenach's cheating treacherous ways. Flodden and all that. Real security only came when you were on terra firma, and sometimes not even then in the ferocious blizzards that passed for the norm hereabouts. Better say safe when that first pint is slithering down your throat in the boozer.

Whymper wouldn't have blinked if he could have seen us, attired splendidly for grouse shooting with Prince Albert, in our hairy breeches, which when wet gave off an aroma redolent of Highland cow pastures. Harnesses were not yet a gleam in Whillan's eye; a rope round the waist tied off with a bowline sufficed, and slow strangulation after a fall was guaranteed, so peeling was no fun. But we saw sunsets to set your heart afire and heard our boots scrunching crisply over the snow on lonely Bens in a Scotland as quiet as of long ago where only ghosts remained in the ruined sheilings in the glens.

So there I was struggling slowly upwards, roasting hot, in my heavy winter clothes, every corner of my being throbbing with fear and the sheer daft pleasure of it all. I was gasping from excitement and effort, picking away at the ice like a bad pointillist painter. Way up above, the gully exit was hidden in the quickening murk with now and again a patch of blue flickering across the cornice, gone in the blink of an eyelid. I glanced up. Two women were standing on the edge of the cornice, waving at us! Jesus! I about jumped out of my britches!

"For Christ's sake get back!" I shouted. That cornice didn't need much of a push to tumble, bringing all four of us to a nasty end. They were women, I could tell because they were waving like they were washing the windows. Men would have give a half-hearted salute, not failing to point out what a *coo's erse* I was making of the step-cutting. Scolded, by the roughness of my tongue they retreated. The blizzard redoubling its efforts, was throwing chunks of ice upwards through the funnel, freezing my face and hands, so I returned to chopping with extra vim, and forgot about them.

The ice pitch finally relented, merging into a steep snow slope. I trudged up the snow, easily bypassing the cornice and rolled over onto the plateau. Then I shoved my axe deep into the snow, tossing my rope round it and called it a belay. Euphoria and relief charged through my veins in a surge of glorious voltage, which not even wet breeches freeze-welding onto the neve could dampen. Brian came up breathing rapidly, so I assumed he was suitably impressed.

"Jeez, man, You chopped these holds out for a ffff..lipping giant!"

"Oh. I forgot you're the dwarf wi' the plastic heid!"

These pleasantries dispensed with, we stuffed our snow covered gear into our sacks, piling in the uncoiled frozen spaghetti of ropes without bothering to dust the frosted rime off of them. But a few steps later we had to haul the ropes out again as we were navigating blind in the midst of a white-out. We were adhering to the theory that if one of us stepped over the edge the other would be able to pull him back from the brink.. The wind knocked us back and forth into each other, making steering like riding a bucking bronco. Taking bearings with the compass was no fun either as the snow hurtling towards us with the velocity of gunfire stung the minute area of flesh on our faces left uncovered. With the rope between us now arched like a bow, now whirring like a crazy skipping rope, we stumbled over the ice-speckled frozen tundra, back down to our frozen slum.

The weather was so miserable that night we went to bed early, but the cold forced us up to make a brew, the stove and the hot drinks managing to drive the temperature fractionally upwards. Eventually we returned to the chill embrace of our sleeping bags, managing to fall asleep till the agitated skier knocked us up early the next morning.

....

The four of us were now spread out into a line along the foot of the Corrie basin facing the great cliffs ahead. I thought it was more realistic to focus my vision on the crest of the plateau, not on the slopes far below. Then I spotted what I had been dreading, a neat V shaped chunk snipped out of the cornice bang in the middle of the cliff line.

Drawing my eyes below, I made out a patch of scuffed up snow, on top of which sat a red snowball the size of a football, and what looked like a grey log lying awkwardly across the slope. I felt a lurch in my stomach. The bleak sight lowered my spirits. Then a curious thing happened.

Approaching the body, I felt I was stepping outside of reality, and watching events unfolding as on a screen. Did the mind unasked for put up a fence, to keep back the dreadful? Or was our own existence so tediously banal that reality only existed through the medium of the small screen? It was the first time I had seen death up close. It could only have been one of the women we saw yesterday.

The others stood around like they were waiting for something. No one wanted to go near to touch the body. The face was down in the snow, totally smothered in ice, so the person was clearly dead. But somebody should check for vital signs, shouldn't they? It was what they did on the telly.

"I suppose we should check for a pulse." They all nodded, but no one moved, looking at me expecting something, "Oh Bollocks!" I stepped forward to inspect the victim. I knelt down in the snow, pulled back her anorak, which together with a thin jumper and blouse was all she wore. I lifted the corner of her blouse, feeling weird and intrusive, as if I were a necrophiliac. The skin felt like marble. If she had been alive I don't know what we would have done, but there was nothing. She was stone cold dead.

My initiative with the corpse somehow put me in charge of the operation. The next thing was to get help. I asked who was the fastest, and the English lad in the middle of a Cairngorm blizzard standing over a recently dead woman, gave me a stride for stride account of his prowess as a cross-country runner, filling me in on all the cups and honors won in case I was inclined to check up. He paused in his eulogy to himself, giving me time to say, "You're the man for the job. Run like the bleedin' wind, and get help. There's two hundred skiers in the next Corrie piddling around on a slope that couldn't harm a fly. Go get 'em!"

He was off like a rocket, ably demonstrating his *resume*, leaving the three of us standing guard over the girl's body. We had time on our hands. Anticipating a long wait we passed the time as if we had just missed the bus and the last one was a long way away. With the gale blowing we had to stand with our mitts against our faces to protect us against the snow pellets stinging our cheeks. We talked about climbing. What else? And as in any situation where words would never be tested, we bragged. We've all done it. Holds recede, slabs are tilted up just a wee bit and the second is hauled up on a fishing line unable to follow our awesome leads. We did the hand ballet familiar in every climber's pub, a lay-back here, a hand jam there, here a jug there a jug.... A few minutes of this usually palls for anyone of voting age, but we hadn't established anything else in common so we kept at it, slapping the air for virtual handholds, while taking breaks to scour the skyline for the stretcher party whenever a patch of blue broke through the murk.

When the rescue team appeared, they were treated to the incongruous sight of the three of us hand jiving over a woman's dead body. Without fuss the body was bundled onto the stretcher, the legs bouncing on the canvas with the stilted gesticulations of a marionette. The fact that none of us appeared to have any curiosity about her or inquired about her name added to the impression that this was just a shell left on the hillside the person inside, whoever she was, long gone.

The clouds parted for the cliff to take a final curtain call, then they drifted away like smoke unfurling until the last particles of mist were nibbled up by the Spey Valley. Framed by a suddenly enormous blue sky the snow glistened and sparkled where the light hit the slope, while the crags, now red, now pink for that moment appeared friendly, making for a scene of beauty, capable of holding anyone for as long as visibility allowed. But to me it was a hideous kind of beauty, a sterile wasteland of indifference, lacking even the pitilessness of the diabolical, more depressing than frightening. I thought then that Mallory was wrong. Nothing is "There."

We were driven down to Aviemore to report to the police. Afterwards the mountain rescue gave us a lift back up to the road end so we could retrieve our gear from the hut. We collected it, swore never to return to this dump and trudged back to the van through the snow. As we were loading up, the sun dropped over the horizon painting on the darkening sky a sunset you might wait for a whole lifetime to see, as if in dying it had thrown a challenge at all the colors of the spectrum. It was the most beautiful thing I had ever seen in nature, but for me it pricked the heart with melancholy.

Just twenty four hours ago another could have shared these feelings. I began wondering about the woman, and not knowing who she was I felt free to adlib. I imagined her enjoying simple things like going to the pictures; throwing clay about in a pottery workshop and having her pals round for a coffee and a blether. She liked to laugh a lot with her own little circle. She had a gift for friendship and was loving, and was loved in return. Now that self-contained little world was switched off. I wished I had been nicer when I shouted at her to stand back. The last words she heard from a stranger were not kind. But then if wishes were horses... I never knew how that saying ended.

"Hurry up, Jimmy, We're freezin!"

"Okay."

The door was shut, the engine chugged ponderously into life, and off we went down into the gloom of the Spey Valley.

Printed in the United States
148696LV00002B/30/P